Protest, Repression and Political Regimes

This volume investigates the relationship between protest, repression and political regimes in Latin America and sub-Saharan Africa.

Considering how different political regimes use repression and respond to popular protest, this book analyses the relationship between protest and repression in Africa and Latin America between the late 1970s and the beginning of the twenty-first century. Drawing on theories, multi-method empirical analyses and case studies, the author of this volume sets out to investigate the reciprocal dynamics between protest and repression. Distinctive features of this volume include:

- quantitative analyses that highlight general trends in the protest–repression relationship
- case studies of different political regimes in Chile and Nigeria, emphasizing the dynamics at the micro level
- an argument for the importance of full democratization in order to reduce the risk, and intensity, of intrastate conflict.

Focusing on political regimes in different areas of the world, *Protest, Repression and Political Regimes* will be of vital interest to students and scholars of conflict studies, human rights and social movements.

Sabine C. Carey is Lecturer in International Relations and Co-Director of ICMCR, University of Nottingham, and Senior Researcher at the Centre for the Study of Civil War at PRIO. Research interests include conflict processes, human rights violations and democratization.

Security and Governance Series
Edited by Fiona B. Adamson
School of Oriental and African Studies, University of London
Roland Paris
University of Ottawa
Stefan Wolff
University of Nottingham

This series reflects the broadening conceptions of security and the growing nexus between the study of governance issues and security issues. The topics covered in the series range from issues relating to the management of terrorism and political violence, non-state actors, transnational security threats, migration, borders and 'homeland security', to questions surrounding weak and failing states, post-conflict reconstruction, the evolution of regional and international security institutions, energy and environmental security, and the proliferation of WMD. Particular emphasis is placed on publishing theoretically informed scholarship that elucidates the governance mechanisms, actors and processes available for managing issues in the new security environment.

Rethinking Japanese Security
Peter J. Katzenstein

**State Building and International
Intervention in Bosnia**
Roberto Belloni

**The UN Security Council and the
Politics of International Authority**
Edited by Bruce Cronin and Ian Hurd

The Dilemmas of Statebuilding
Confronting the contradictions of
postwar peace operations
*Edited by Roland Paris and
Timothy D. Sisk*

**Protest, Repression and
Political Regimes**
An empirical analysis of Latin America
and sub-Saharan Africa
Sabine C. Carey

First published 2009 by Routledge
2 Park Square, Milton Park, Abingdon, Oxfordshire OX14 4RN

Simultaneously published in the USA and Canada
by Routledge
711 Third Avenue, New York, NY 10017

First issued in paperback 2014

Routledge is an imprint of the Taylor & Francis Group, an informa business

© 2009 Sabine C. Carey

Typeset in Sabon by
RefineCatch Limited, Bungay, Suffolk

British Library Cataloguing in Publication Data
A catalogue record for this book is available from the British Library

Library of Congress Cataloging in Publication Data
A catalog record for this book has been requested

ISBN 13: 978–1–138–87451–0 (pbk)
ISBN 13: 978–0–415–42484–4 (hbk)

Protest, Repression and Political Regimes

An empirical analysis of Latin America and sub-Saharan Africa

Sabine C. Carey

Routledge
Taylor & Francis Group

LONDON AND NEW YORK

This book is dedicated to the memory of Steve Poe

Contents

Figures

Tables

Acknowledgements

The research for this book has been supported by the Economic and Social Research Council, the Leverhulme Trust, the German Academic Exchange Service (DAAD) and the Methods and Data Institute at the University of Nottingham. I am grateful to Sage Publishing for permission to reuse the material of an article I published in *Political Research Quarterly* in 2006. I could not have written this book without the input and support of many people. I am particularly grateful to David Sanders, who has guided my work on this project from its earliest stages. His sharp mind and meticulous effort to improve my work was invaluable for the end product. Hugh Ward and Ken Benoit provided essential input and encouraged me to turn this project into a book. I am grateful to Will Lowe for his patience in endless discussions about methodological and statistical questions. The advice and support I received from Stefan Wolff was essential towards the final stages. My parents enabled me, in so many ways, to write this book and my two boys gave me the energy to complete it. Last, but certainly not least, I am more grateful to my husband Sean than I can put in words. This book is dedicated to the memory of Steve Poe, who was the best mentor, role model and friend I could have hoped for.

Abbreviations

AC	Asamblea de la Civilidad (Assembly of Civil Society)
AD	Alianza Democrática (Democratic Alliance)
CD	Campaign for Democracy
CNI	Centro Nacional de Información (National Information Centre)
CTC	Confederación de Trabajadores del Cobre (Copper Workers' Confederation)
DINA	Dirección Nacional de Inteligencia (Directorate of National Intelligence)
FPMR	Frente Patriótico Manuel Rodríguez (Manuel Rodriguez Patriotic Front)
ING	Interim National Government
IPI	Intranational Political Interactions
IYC	Ijaw Youth Council
MDC	Movement for Democratic Change
MDP	Movimiento Democrático Popular (Democratic Popular Movement)
MOSOP	Movement for the Survival of the Ogoni People
NADECO	National Democratic Coalition
NRC	National Republican Convention
PCCH	Partido Comunista de Chile (Chilean Communist Party)
PTS	Political Terror Scale
SAP	Structural Adjustment Programmes
SDP	Social Democratic Party
VAR	Vector Autoregression

1 Introduction

Instances in which attacks from the opposition are met by violent attacks from the state, or examples of civil society protesting against a repressive government, can be found from all around the globe. President Robert Mugabe of Zimbabwe has increasingly used repression, torture and political imprisonment to silence his opponents and to intimidate potential protesters against his regime; any calls for strikes by the main opposition party are immediately silenced by security forces. In 2002, a major strike organized by labour unions, industrial magnates and oil workers in Venezuela against President Chavez, resulted in the firing of the management of the state-run petroleum company and the dismissal of thousands of its employees, but overall comparatively limited violence was used to end this form of dissent. In Tibet during March 2008, Buddhist monks demonstrated peacefully against religious restrictions by Chinese authorities. Chinese security forces arrested large numbers of the protesters, which further escalated the display of dissent. This, in turn, led to the escalation of violence between the Tibetan protesters and Chinese police.

Looking at these conflicts, several questions arise. How do governments respond to popular protest? When do governments respond with violence to their citizens protesting, particularly when this protest is peaceful? How does a violent government crackdown influence the dynamics of the protest? Does government repression increase protest and the risk of rebellions? Is the interaction between the government and the opposition different under different political regimes? These are the main questions addressed in this book. It investigates the relationship between protest and repression in Latin America and sub-Saharan Africa.

The question whether domestic protest leads to repressive or cooperative behaviour of the government and its security forces is important not only for the dissidents and protesters themselves, but also for national and international actors who try to mediate conflicts between the government and the opposition. If domestic protest triggers state cooperation, then the display of discontent is no reason for severe concerns about its consequences. However, if the display of opposition leads to a tighter grip by the government on actual and potential opponents, then steps to intervene and mediate the situation should be taken at the first signs of domestic dissent. For example, prior, during and after the general elections in Zimbabwe in March 2008, students and members of the opposition party Movement for Democratic Change (MDC) staged various protests and rallies against President Mugabe. The response of the government, however, was clear: it intimidated opposition supporters with the use of widespread violence, further limited the freedom of the press and generally tightened its grip on power. The question is whether these immediate retaliatory actions are a typical pattern of state–societal relations and whether the dynamics of these interactions differ under different circumstances.

This book analyses the relationship between domestic protest and state repression in Africa and Latin America between the late 1970s and the beginning of the twenty-first century. It sheds light on how domestic dissent and state coercion respond to each other. The main question addressed in this book is whether domestic protest triggers state coercion and whether state coercion triggers domestic protest. It empirically analyses whether the dynamics of domestic conflict differ between democracies, semi-democracies and non-democracies, and whether there are geographically distinct patterns of interaction by comparing countries from sub-Saharan Africa and Latin America.

Figure 1.1 graphically displays the relationships that are the focus of this book. I investigate how dissent influences repression, and how state coercion impacts upon actions of dissent. Particular attention is paid to how, if at all, the nature of this protest–repression nexus differs under different political regimes, focusing on the degree of democracy as the core characteristic. Finally, I investigate how the degree of democracy influences the use of violence by governments and the protest behaviour of the population. To explore the relationships shown graphically in Figure 1.1 from different angles, I use a mixed-method form of analysis, employing quantitative and qualitative methods. The initial analysis is conducted at the macro level.

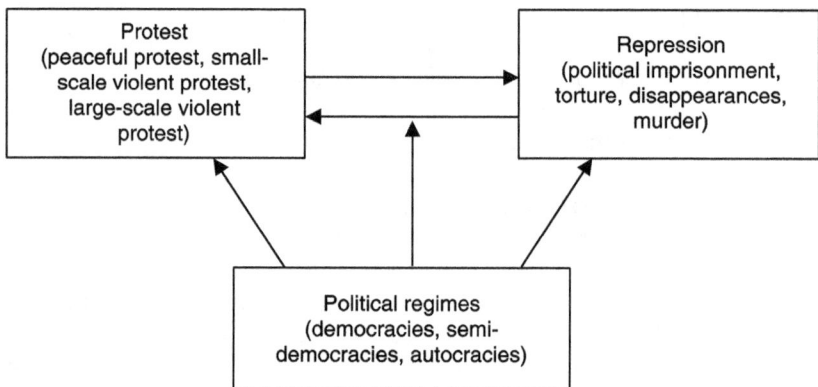

Figure 1.1 A model of protest, repression and political regimes.

It employs ordered probit models to analyse yearly data from 66 Latin American and sub-Saharan African countries between 1977 and 2002. The analysis differentiates between different types of dissent (peaceful dissent, riots and large-scale violent dissent) and different degrees of repression. It demonstrates how these types of protest affect repression, and how repression influences protest. The analyses also examine the impact of regime type on both protest and repression, controlling for political instability, civil war, population size and regional differences between Latin America and Africa. These general analyses are complemented with a series of individual time-series analyses with daily data from six Latin American and three African countries. The main contribution of this second set of statistical analyses is that it specifically models the reciprocal dynamics between protest and repression. It extends the definition of these two concepts to include verbal behaviour and incorporates accommodating actions into the analysis of domestic conflict. These two quantitative approaches are complemented by two case studies, of Chile and Nigeria. They provide a historical narrative to the protest–repression nexus, and add a further, in-depth dimension to the picture that is outlined by the statistical analyses.

In the remainder of this chapter, I present theories and hypotheses commonly found in the literature. I first focus on research that views the state as being reactive and investigates how governments respond to protest. Then I discuss the main arguments that have been developed on how the use of repression influences protest behaviour. In each of these sections I discuss how political regimes in general, and democracy in particular, have been found to influence both protest and repression.

When we consider instances where citizens have voiced their discontent with the ruling government in various shapes and forms, governments are generally keen to put an end to the show of dissent. Sometimes, governments act with restraint, while at other times government forces unleash extreme and widespread violence against the protesters, and even against bystanders and the wider population. The question is when do governments use violence and repression as a response to dissent? The following section discusses the main reasons why governments use repression as a response to dissent.

Internal unrest is generally found to increase repression (Davenport 1995; Tilly 1978). Past research has shown strong support for the argument that countries are more likely to suffer from torture, extrajudicial killings and political imprisonment during times of civil war (e.g. Krain 1997; Poe and Tate 1994; Zanger 2000), where civil war is an extreme example of instability and popular resistance. More generally, the empirical literature has provided substantial support for the argument that dissent, such as in the form of strikes, demonstrations or guerrilla warfare, increases the use of state coercion (Davenport 2005; Davis and Ward 1990; Gupta *et al.* 1993; Gurr and Lichbach 1986; Poe *et al.* 1999; Regan and Henderson 2002). The main theoretical reason that has been presented for violent government responses to dissent activities is that the authorities resort to violence in order to restore their political control by extinguishing dissent. Unrest and protest are perceived as a threat to government authority and legitimacy, therefore governments use force to strengthen their position and to eliminate the threat (Boudreau 2005; Davenport 1995; Poe 2004). Dissent – particularly violent forms of protest – is often interpreted by governments as sufficient justification for the use of force in order to restore 'law and order' (Davenport 2007a).

Mason (2004) suggests that governments in developing countries often respond with a disproportional amount of violence to non-violent collective action because institutional mechanisms for accommodating grievances are missing or underdeveloped. Davenport (1995) argues that governments distinguish between different forms of threat when they employ negative sanctions. He finds that governments increase the level of sanctions when faced with a higher number of dissent activities, when different forms of protest are employed, and when the activities lie outside the norms of interaction in that country. Analysing government and dissident behaviour in Peru and Sri Lanka, Moore argues that 'states tended to substitute accommodation for repression and repression for accommodation whenever either tactic was met with dissent' (2000: 120). Gartner and Regan (1996) find that government repression does not always increase proportionally with increasing dissent. Their study of 18 Latin American countries suggests that as the demands of the dissidents increase, governments react with more restraint. Additionally, governments appear to overreact to relatively low demands with violent coercion.

Not all governments respond to dissent in the same way. For example, when shantytown dwellers in Chile illegally seized land in 1983 under the military regime of General Pinochet, they were arrested and severely repressed by the security forces of the military junta. Six years later, after the democratic election of President Aylwin, shantytown dwellers again seized land illegally, but this time the reaction consisted of verbal condemnation, not violent coercion (Hipsher 1996). Clearly, the nature of the political regime has an important influence on a government's use of repression. Political regimes reflect the norms that guide political interactions and the institutions through which those interactions are channelled. They determine the levels of power and force that can legitimately be used against citizens, and facilitate the accommodation of opposition grievances. Democracies are generally associated with non-violence (Rummel 1997). Democracy

> institutionalizes a way of solving without violence disagreements over fundamental questions. Democracy promotes a culture of negotiation, bargaining, compromise, concession, the tolerance of differences, and even the acceptance of defeat . . . And it unleashes forces that divide and segment the sources of violence.
>
> (Rummel 1997: 101)

In short, in a democracy, norms and institutions are in place that make it less likely for governments to resort to violence against their own citizens. Democratic political institutions facilitate the inclusion of opposition groups and provide legitimate channels for regime opponents to voice their discontent in non-violent ways. At the same time, they provide the government with tools and procedures to engage with the opposition in a peaceful and institutionalized framework. Therefore, democratic institutions render opposition grievances less threatening, reducing the incentives for governments to react harshly to dissent. Democratic institutions also attach a high cost to state coercion. A government is less likely to employ violence against its citizens if it needs the support of the general public in order to be re-elected into office. At the same time, democratic norms lower the willingness of all actors to resort to violence in solving disagreements and conflicts between the ruling government and potential dissidents.

While most studies agree that dissent provokes government coercion, particularly in non-democratic countries, the picture is less clear when we turn the relationship around and ask how state coercion influences protest.

There is an abundance of contradictory theorizing and empirical evidence about whether state repression increases or decreases the incidence of social protest.[1] Zimmerman summarizes the situation as follows:

> There are two contradictory expectations about the effect of governmental coercion on protest and rebellion: coercion either will deter them or will instigate people to higher levels of conflict behaviour. . . . Thus there are theoretical arguments for all conceivable basic relations between governmental coercion and group protest and rebellion except for no relationship.
>
> (Zimmerman 1980: 191)

Over two decades since Zimmerman's evaluation, the picture of the repression–protest nexus has not become substantially clearer. Davenport calls for 'the replication of analyses within diverse contexts' (2005: x), the use of diverse methodologies and datasets in order to advance our knowledge on how repression impacts upon dissent. This book addresses some of those concerns by applying complementary methodological approaches to investigate different sets of data that cover a range of different contexts. It employs three types of empirical investigation of the protest–repression nexus in Latin America and Africa. The first analysis examines the relationship between protest and repression on a macro level, using yearly data from 43 countries from sub-Saharan Africa and 23 countries from Latin America between 1977 and 2002. The main advantage of this analysis is that it provides information about the general nature of this relationship in these two regions, while controlling for important variables. The second analysis focuses on the dynamics of the relationship by investigating daily data from six Latin American and three African countries. The two main contributions of this second analysis are that it specifically models the interdependence between protest and repression, and that it includes cooperative behaviour in the analysis of domestic conflict. The final analysis focuses on the micro level. It presents two illustrative case studies, one of Chile and one of Nigeria, to show how the interactions between government and non-government actors have played out in specific circumstances. These qualitative case studies allow tracing the causal chain in more detail compared to the quantitative analyses.

The main theories that explain how state repression influences protest and rebellion can be divided into two broad categories: theories that are based on psychological factors, such as perception of inequality by potential rebels, and those that focus on rational behaviour, either of the individual or of groups, in terms of mobilizing structures.[2]

Relative deprivation theory has been widely used to explain and predict domestic rebellion and dissent (e.g. Davies 1962; Ellina and Moore 1990; Gurr 1968, 1970; Muller 1980; Muller and Weede 1994). The main argument of this theory is that people who feel deprived relative to their expectations are more likely to protest and rebel against the regime. Gurr argues that '[d]iscontent arising from the perception of relative deprivation is that basic, instigating condition for participants in collective violence' (1970: 13).[3] The main cause for social dissent is the frustration of people, not cost–benefit calculations or mobilization by leaders. Gurr outlines that

> the primary source of the human capacity for violence appears to be the frustration–aggression mechanism. . . . If frustrations are sufficiently prolonged or sharply felt, aggression is quite likely, if not certain, to occur. . . . The frustration–aggression mechanism is in this sense analogous to the law of gravity: men who are frustrated have an innate disposition to do violence to its source in proportion to the intensity of their frustration.
>
> (Gurr 1970: 36–7)

Frustration is defined as 'a discrepancy between value expectations and value capabilities, where value expectations are the amount of important goods and conditions of life to which people feel rightfully entitled and value capabilities are their assessment of what they actually have' (Muller and Weede 1994: 41). Relative deprivation creates anger, which leads to protest. Looking at the relationship between repression and dissent, relative deprivation theory predicts that repression increases protest, where repression is perceived as depriving citizens of their right to be free from coercive actions by the state. Relative deprivation theory is, at its core, a psychological theory.[4] It uses people's frustration levels to determine their proneness to rebel against the political regime.[5]

As Mason points out, relative deprivation theory generally over-predicts dissent and revolution (Mason 2004: 35). In many countries, at many points in time, many people have felt frustrated about their political or economic situations, and perceived themselves to be substantially worse off compared to their own expectations, yet rebellions or revolutions have been relatively rare events. Focusing on civil war and rebellion, Collier (2000) points out that even if people feel deprived relative to their expectations or are frustrated with an unjust regime, they would need to overcome the problem of collective action to organize potential rebels (Lichbach 1995; Olson 1993). Therefore, the greed of individuals needs to be instrumentalized in order to organize a rebellion. Collier (2000) argues that rebels can be motivated by greed, by accumulating private wealth and resources in illegal ways during conflict. Without the opportunity to satisfy individual greed, rebellion is not expected to take place (Collier and Hoeffler 2004; Fearon and Laitin 2003).

Several theories have focused on the problem of collective action for dissent. In the following, I introduce resource mobilization theory, which focuses on the organizational processes of protest mobilization, before discussing the main arguments of micromobilization theory, which also concentrates on mobilizing structures, but at the individual instead of the organizational level.

Resource mobilization theory concentrates on the processes by which citizens are mobilized to participate in protest movements.[6] In contrast to relative deprivation theory, which predicts individuals will rebel when they are frustrated about the political regime, resource mobilization does not utilize feelings, such as anger, as the main motivation behind domestic dissent. Resource mobilization perceives rebels as comparing social costs and benefits from participating in such a movement. McCarthy and Zald argue that, 'there is sensitivity to the importance of costs and rewards in explaining individual and organizational involvement in social movement activity. Costs and rewards are centrally affected by the structure of society and the activities of authorities' (1977: 1216). Resource mobilization models focus on organizational processes by emphasizing 'the significance of organizational bases, resource accumulation, and collective coordination for popular political actors' (McAdam *et al.* 2001: 15). They expect that dense social networks are more likely to develop a social movement than a loose, or non-existent, network.[7]

Micromobilization theory is similar to resource mobilization models. But whereas the latter focus on movement organizations and the use of elite resources, micromobilization theory concentrates on the individual and on personal ties instead of the organizational level (Macy 1991; Marwell and Oliver 1993; Rasler 1996). Micromobilization theory argues that potential rebels can be mobilized for opposition movements by overt dissident behaviour because this (a) shows the willingness and commitment of others, (b) makes the goal of their activities desirable and (c) raises the social rewards for participating in this movement (Chong 1991). Mobilizing structures play a crucial role in this process. They are defined as 'those collective vehicles, informal as well as formal, through which people mobilise and engage in collective action' (McAdam *et al.* 1996: 3). Mobilizing structures can be established networks, such as labour or student unions, while the level of urbanization also influences the costs of engaging in collective actions.

Micromobilization theory predicts different effects of repression on social protest, depending on the circumstances. In the short run, repression is expected to increase the costs of protest and hence decreases protest (McAdam *et al.* 1996). In the long run, however, 'repression sets in motion "micromobilization processes" that raise the rewards and diminish the costs of participation' (Opp and Roehl 1990: 523). Hence, repression has direct negative, but indirect positive effects on social protest movements.

The importance of believing in the success of protest is picked up by the expected utility approach. This approach argues that

> rebellious political behaviour is a purposeful form of contention for political power and, therefore, that no matter how frustrated people are by conditions of relative deprivation, they will not contend collectively for political power by means of rebellion unless the likelihood of success of rebellion is high and the expected benefits of rebellion exceed the expected costs.
>
> (Muller and Weede 1994: 41).[8]

Similar to other branches of rational actor models, expected utility theory argues that individuals, in this case the rebels or dissidents, weigh the costs and benefits of their actions. It emphasizes that people will engage in collective protest only if they expect it to bring about the desired end.

This book combines two major strands of research: one investigates the impact of dissent on repression and the other the influence of repression on dissent. To date, there is little research that explicitly addresses both directions of the relationship between protest and repression.[9] To analyse the protest–repression nexus in the context of Latin America and sub-Saharan Africa, I employ a multi-method approach, using macro-level, meso-level and micro-level analyses to further our understanding of the interactions between the government and the opposition.

To date, there has been no systematic comparison of the protest–repression nexus between different geographical areas. This monograph compares the results obtained from African countries with those from Latin American countries, in order to separate general characteristics of the relationship between protest and repression from geographically specific patterns. Additionally, I argue that the relationship between the state and the population is likely to differ between democracies, semi-democracies and non-democracies. Political regimes set the stage for the interaction between the state and its citizens. It shapes the behaviour of both sets of actors. Therefore, I investigate the interaction between protest and repression under different institutional settings.

The remainder of this book is structured as follows. Chapter 2 defines the core concepts used in the study and clarifies the conceptualization of the actors that are focus of the empirical analyses. It develops a model of domestic political conflict and derives hypotheses, which are empirically tested in the subsequent chapters. The model presents the argument that protest increases the risk of repression and, vice versa, that repression increases the risk of protest. It further refines the argument by distinguishing between violent and non-violent dissent, different levels of repression and different types of political regime. These theoretical arguments are subjected to macro-level analyses in Chapter 3. The analysis uses ordered probit models to statistically test the hypotheses developed in the preceding chapter with yearly data from 66 Latin American and sub-Saharan African countries from 1977–2002. The results confirm that conflictual behaviour of one actor leads to conflictual behaviour of the other. They also show that the most important feature of dissent, from the perspective of the government, is, whether the dissent activity is violent or not, where violent dissent is perceived to be more threatening than non-violent demonstrations and strikes. The results also show that democracy lowers the risk of repression, even when governments are faced with dissent. But while democracy seems to be an effective way of reducing the risk of state coercion, it has no impact upon dissident behaviour.

Chapter 4 builds upon the theoretical model presented in Chapter 2 and develops it further. It focuses specifically on the dynamics between pro-test and repression. Chapter 4 also adds cooperative behaviour into the equation of protest and repression. Previous research has largely focused on conflictual behaviour. In Chapter 4, I address the question of whether repression successfully leads the opposition to more cooperative behaviour, and whether strikes and riots are a useful tool for minimizing coercion exer-cised by the state. To investigate the arguments put forward in Chapter 4, I use the data from the Intranational Political Interaction (IPI) project (Davis *et al.* 1998; Moore 1998, 2000). These daily data measure conflictual and accommodating behaviours by government and non-government actors. This dataset consists of information on six Latin American and three sub-Saharan African countries (Argentina, Brazil, Chile, Colombia, Mexico, Venezuela, Nigeria, Zaire[10] and Zimbabwe) between the late 1970s and early 1990s. In Chapter 5, I utilize vector autoregression (VAR) models to test the potentially reciprocal relationship between protest and repression, using the IPI data.[11] In the analysis, I distinguish between democracies, semi-democracies and autocracies, to investigate whether the dynamics between protest and repression differ under different political regimes. The results largely confirm the findings of the macro-analysis from Chapter 3. Both protest and repression reinforce each other and have self-perpetuating effects. But this time-series analysis also shows that democracies are no less likely than other regimes to use repression in response to dissent. While accommodating behaviour of both the government and the opposition is not completely explained by the models, the results suggest that in authoritarian regimes accommodating actions by one actor are exploited by conflictual behaviour of the other actor.

In Chapter 6, I present a third set of analyses to add to the picture drawn from the statistical results from Chapters 3 and 5. The empirical investigation in this penultimate chapter is located on the micro level, using two case studies to illustrate the dynamics between protest and repression. To show how the interactions between a government and the opposition can play out, I outline the main dynamics of the protest–repression nexus in Chile from the beginning of Pinochet's military rule in 1973 to the return to democracy in 1988, and in Nigeria during military rule from 1983 to 1999 and the beginning of the Fourth Republic under the civilian President Olusegun Obasanjo. The case studies highlight that while repression tends to lead to protest, as suggested by the results of the statistical analyses in the earlier chapters, particularly violent and indiscriminate repression tends to create a climate of fear and intimidation, which effectively stifles open protest and dissent. The two case studies in comparison also emphasize the importance of strong and independent political parties, as these can play a crucial role in mobilizing civil society against an authoritarian regime, which was the case in Chile. In Nigeria, on the other hand, the decades of military rule, combined with corruption, neopatrimonialism and poverty made the leadership of the opposition open to co-optation by the military junta. These micro-level studies also illustrate how important a strong democratic past and tradition is, which can be built upon after the end of a military regime. After the election of President Alfonsin ended the military rule of General Pinochet in 1988, Chile could return to a democratic system, while the end of military rule in Nigeria in 1999 left the country with a semi-democracy with weak political institutions. As a result, dissent in Chile moved from taking place outside of the political system, as was the case under military rule, to being expressed primarily within the democratic institutions provided by the political regime. In the Nigerian semi-democracy, however, communal violence and militant actions against the state became even more severe as the level of threat experienced under the Abacha regime declined.

In sum, this book tries to fill that gap in the literature on the important issue of the relationship between protest and repression. It addresses the following questions: Does protest lead to repression? Does repression lead to protest? And do the answers to these two questions differ between democracies, semi-democracies and non-democracies, as well as between Latin America and sub-Saharan Africa? These questions are explored using three different methodological approaches on different levels of analyses aggregation in order to provide rich and new insights into the relationship between protest and repression.

Notes

1 See, for example, Davenport *et al.* 2005; Francisco 1995, 1996; Gupta *et al.* 1993; Gurr 1986; Hibbs 1973; Lichbach 1987; Mason 2004; Moore 1998; Opp 1994; Opp and Roehl 1990; Rasler 1996; Tilly 1978; Weinstein 2007; Zimmerman 1980.
2 See Mason (2004) for an excellent and detailed review of these theories, which are categorized in a slightly different way than above.
3 The backlash hypothesis, which is not always used with an explicit connection to a theoretical framework, resembles this. The backlash hypothesis argues that 'harsh coercion accelerates protest' (Francisco 1996: 1182). It predicts that extremely harsh repression, particularly when applied indiscriminately, increases rebellion (see also Mason and Krane 1989).
4 For further details of the psychological aspects of relative deprivation theory, see Rule (1988).
5 Relative deprivation theory also highlights other factors, apart from repression, that play an important role in determining the levels of domestic dissent. Economic discrimination and political separatism are the main indicators for persisting deprivation, whereas inflation rates and export values are used as measures for short-term deprivation (Gurr 1970; Muller and Weede 1994; Rule 1988). Deprivation theory also identifies mediating factors, which are mainly conflict tradition, party system stability and regime coerciveness (Gurr 1970; Rule 1988).
6 Resource mobilization theory is not always classified as a rational actor approach. I categorize it as a rational actor model because actors are not perceived as being driven by psychological factors, such as grievances, but they compare the costs and benefits of their actions and organizational structures play a crucial role, similar to other rational actor approaches. Classifications that do not list resource mobilization theory as a rational actor model usually emphasize the psychological aspects of this approach, stressing the role of ideologies and identities in mobilizing social movements (Klandermans 1997; Oberschall 1993). Examples of resource mobilization studies are Khawaja (1994), Klandermans (1984), McAdam *et al.* (1996, 1997), Opp (1994) and Tarrow (1995).
7 For a detailed critique of the resource mobilization theory, see Piven and Cloward (1995).
8 Muller and Weede label this 'power contention theory' (1994: 41). On the individual level, this approach is usually referred to as value expectancy model, which argues that 'people will rebel if they become convinced that dissent will achieve the collective good' (Rasler 1996: 134).
9 For example, see Carey (2006) and Davis and Ward (1990).
10 I use the country name Zaire, as the name changed to the Democratic Republic of Congo only in 1997, whereas the time-series analysis ends in 1992.
11 The analysis in this chapter is based on Carey (2006). I am grateful to Sage Publications for permission to reuse the material.

2 Domestic conflict and political regimes

This chapter outlines the dynamics between protest, repression and political regimes. It discusses how repression and protest influence each other, and how the characteristics of this relationship are expected to differ in different political systems. The first part of this chapter defines the main phenomena of domestic political conflict, repression and protest. The second part develops a theory of domestic conflict and derives hypotheses that are tested in the following chapters.

DEFINING DOMESTIC POLITICAL CONFLICT

Social conflict has been defined as 'a struggle over values or claims to status, power, and scarce resources, in which the aims of the conflict groups are not only to gain the desired values, but also to neutralize, injure, and eliminate rivals' (Coser 1967: 232). It is a struggle over influence and power. I argue that this struggle is, in general, a zero-sum game. The gains of one actor are the losses of another. The increase of power and influence usually comes at the cost of the decreased power and influence of another actor. In the following, I focus on *political* conflict, on the struggle over power and resources that rival groups typically engage in. I assume that both protesters and the state attempt to increase their influence and control over political issues, and try to weaken the opponent.

Gurr and Lichbach define political conflict as 'open physical confrontations between collective actors over political issues' (1986: 5). Based on this definition, political conflict has three main elements: (1) actions, which are (2) fuelled by political issues and (3) carried out by collective actors. I impose the additional criterion that the collective actors must be domestic actors. For example, confrontational acts by foreign politicians or by foreign media are not part of the concept of political conflict as it is understood within this context. For the purpose of this book, domestic political conflict is defined as confrontation by domestic actors over political issues. In this sense, domestic political conflict includes, but is not restricted to, 'sustained, conflictual interaction between social challengers and opponents' (Tilly 1984: 299).[1]

I focus on two actors, the state and the opposition. Two assumptions are made about them. First, they are assumed to be unitary actors. Although there are often different groups within the state that favour different tactics – for example, hardliners might prefer to pursue to violent strategies, while softliners are more willing to collaborate with the opposition – the state is interested in protecting, or expanding, its sphere of power and influence. It is united in its aim to stay in power and to diminish the threat from potential or actual opponents of the state (Crescenzi 1999; Lichbach 1987; Sutter 1995; Swaminathan 1999). The assumption that the state is a unitary actor, however, does not always reflect the true relationship among state forces across time and space. In many cases, it is exactly the split among the ruling elite that brings about domestic conflict.[2] The opposition is also viewed as a unitary actor that is interested in extending, or at least in defending, its power. It aims at challenging, and sometimes even at overthrowing, the rulers. While there might be divisions between opposition groups as well, they are assumed to be united in their goals, namely in wanting to maintain or improve their status quo.[3] The core interest of this study is the relationship between the government and domestic opposition, not the dynamics within the ruling class of a country or within various rebel groups and regime opponents. Within this framework, the assumption that the government and the opposition are unitary actors is a helpful instrument to reduce the complexity of reality in order to focus on the dynamics that drive the conflict between the state and its opponents.

The domestic opposition incorporates all domestic actors that are not part of the state apparatus. It includes dissident organizations, such as guerrilla groups, labour unions, students, churches and opposition parties, but also members of the general population and ethnic groups. The concept of the opposition is therefore not restricted to organized rebels or dissidents. Nevertheless, to avoid repetition, the terms 'dissidents', 'rebels', 'opposition' and 'population' are used interchangeably, having the same broad meaning as outlined above. The state as unitary actor includes the national executive, the judiciary and elected representatives, as well as local government, political parties in power, military, police and other paramilitary forces of the government.

The second assumption is that both actors are rational (e.g. Chong 1991; Lichbach 1995; Mason 2004; Oberschall 1994; Taylor 1998). The emphasis is on the political process, not on deprivation, frustration or grievances (Gurr 1968). Dissident activities are seen as a reaction to government behaviour, and governments respond as rational actors to the challenges that are posed by the dissidents. Within this framework, domestic political conflict is an inherently dynamic and reciprocal process, where reciprocity is 'the behaviour of one actor . . . conditioned by the behaviour of other actors in a given social system' (Moore 1995: 133). The government reacts to threats exercised through various protest activities, and the population responds to repression and negative sanctions by the government.

Protest is defined as 'disruptive collective action that is aimed at institutions, elites, authorities, or other groups on behalf of the collective goals of the actors or of those they claim to represent' (Tarrow 1991: 11). Throughout this book, the terms 'protest' and 'dissent' are used interchangeably to mean any kind of resistance to the government, unless the nature of dissent, or protest, is further specified to be of violent or non-violent nature, for example. Government repression is understood as the violation of the human right to physical integrity, or life integrity violations. Howard and Donnelly state that

> [i]ndividuals – regardless of who they are or where they stand – have the inherent dignity and moral worth that the state must not merely passively respect, but for which it must demonstrate an active concern. Furthermore, everyone is *entitled* to this equal concern and respect.
>
> (Howard and Donnelly 1986: 803)

This book focuses on instances in which governments did not respect the 'inherent dignity and worth' of each individual, but used repression against its people. Gurr characterizes state terrorism generally as 'coercive, life-threatening action' (1986: 46). This conceptualization of state terrorism focuses on the violation of basic life integrity rights. The violation of basic life integrity rights, or personal integrity rights, includes torture, imprisonment, politically motivated murder and disappearances (e.g. Henderson 1991; Mitchell and McCormick 1988; Poe and Tate 1994; Zanger 2000). To minimize repetition, I use the terms human rights violations, life integrity violations, repression and coercion interchangeably.

The following two sections elaborate on the relationship between dissent and repression. First, I conceptualize the state as being reactive, responding to domestic dissent activities. The second section turns the causal arrow around and explains how state coercion influences domestic dissent. In both sections, particular attention is given to how political regimes influence both dissent and repression, and how regimes shape the impact of protest and repression on one another. Chapter 4 builds upon these arguments and further extends them to conceptualize the protest–repression nexus specifically as a dynamic and reciprocal relationship.

USING REPRESSION TO DETER DISSENT

The main argument for using dissident movement as the independent and the regime's behaviour as the dependent variable is that the regime is assumed to maintain the status quo until the status quo is challenged. If there are no challenges to the status quo, the ruling elites have no incentive to move from their position and to change their behaviour. The common hypothesis is that, the greater the threat posed by the opposition, the more likely it is that the regime will respond with repression (e.g. Davis and Ward 1990), hence a positive linear relationship is expected. This relationship has also found consistent support in the quantitative literature (e.g. Davenport 2007a; Krain 1997; Poe 2004; Poe *et al.* 1999; Regan and Henderson 2002). Governments intend to maintain, or improve, the strength:threat ratio. From the point of view of the government, the strength of the state should always be greater than the threat posed by the opposition. Hence, if a threat in the form of popular protest increases, the state is expected to respond either by increasing its strength or by diminishing the threat. The threat leads to insecurity among the ruling elites. In order to regain power and control, which was weakened by domestic protest, the government exercises its strength to reduce the threat in the form of repression and coercion. Repression is used

> as a regulatory mechanism. Specifically, repression is viewed as a strategic choice made by government authorities in an effort to decrease dissident domestic threats, the application of which is influenced by the type, scope, and intensity of the threat presented (repressive opportunity structure) as well as different contextual factors: the preparedness and character of the military, ideology, and regime type.
>
> (Davenport 2000: 9)

From this, follows the general hypothesis:

H_1: Dissent increases the probability of repression.

Yet different protest strategies might have different effects on government behaviour. For example, Davenport (1995) finds that the violence of dissent does not affect state repression, while the strategic variety of dissent activities, frequency of events and deviation from a norm increase coercion. In a study of 18 Latin American countries between 1977 and 1986, Gartner and Regan (1996) came to the conclusion that governments overreact to relatively low levels of dissent and respond with more restraint as dissent increases. It seems reasonable to expect that while governments increase repression in the face of dissent, they do so at different levels of intensity, depending on the type of dissent they are confronted with. A gang of youths who boycott government policies by burning cars and throwing bottles into shop windows, are unlikely to face the same kind of response as organized guerrilla groups that stage an enduring and violent campaign against the rulers. For example, during the riots that followed the Kenyan election in 2007, police were firing guns into the crowds, and used tear gas to disperse opposition forces that were throwing stones and using machetes against members of the president's ethnic group. This kind of government response is not on the same level as the responses that governments used in reaction to the peasant revolution in El Salvador or the Shining Path's guerrilla warfare in Peru during the 1980s.

If dissent is peaceful – for example, if it takes place in the form of peaceful anti-government demonstrations or strikes – it seems likely that governments might react with more restraint than if they were faced with large-scale guerrilla warfare. Violent dissent activities are perceived to be more threatening than non-violent behaviour, hence triggering a more severe response from the government. If protesters resort to violence, this indicates particularly high levels of discontent and willingness on their part to use extreme measures in order to make their point. The use of violence by opposition forces also undermines the government's authority over the sole use of force, and undermines its ability to provide and maintain security within its borders. This puts pressure on the government to end the violent dissent swiftly and effectively, making it more tempting for the government to employ extreme measures. Thus:

> $H_{1.1}$: Violent forms of dissent are more likely to increase repression compared to non-violent forms of dissent.

But, as the study by Gartner and Regan (1996) mentioned above suggests, there might not always be this linear relationship between dissent and government repression, where more severe dissent leads to more repressive state reactions. I argue that the nature of the political regime, in particular the degree of democracy of the political institutions, shapes governments' responses to dissent. This argument is explored more fully in the following section.

DEMOCRACY AND REPRESSION

The response of the government to dissident activities is influenced by various factors besides dissent. Of particular interest here is the political regime within which a government and its opposition operate. Lawson defines a political regime as 'the formal and informal organization of the centre of political power, and of its relations with the broader society. A regime determines who has access to power, and how those who are in power deal with those who are not' (1993: 185). Kitschelt offers a similar definition, arguing that political regimes are 'rules and basic political resource allocations according to which actors exercise authority by imposing and enforcing collective decisions on a bounded constituency' (1992: 1028). Both definitions highlight their role in laying the ground rules for political governance and power allocation. They describe political systems, not specific governments.

Political regimes set the rules of the game and shape the relationship between the government and the opposition. They determine the choices the actors make and the costs that are attached to those choices. For example, particularly in poor authoritarian regimes, there are often no institutionalized channels that deal with popular discontent and opposition (Mason 2004). The norms and institutions that are in place in democracies, on the other hand, are designed to handle political conflict and confrontation peacefully, and to facilitate compromise and cooperation. This is expected to keep the level of conflict low compared to non-democratic regimes.

There is a large body of work that investigates the impact of political regime characteristics on state repression, supporting the argument that democracies are less likely to use repression, since democratic norms and institutions provide non-violent channels for conflict settlement (e.g. Colaresi and Carey 2008; Davenport 2007a, 2007b; Mitchell and McCormick 1988; Poe and Tate 1994; Zanger 2000). Davenport and Armstrong (2004) argue that there is a high threshold of the degree of democracy, above which there is a negative linear relationship with repression, but below this threshold, the degree of democracy has no influence on the level of repression. Their research suggests that countries need to have thoroughly institutionalized democratic procedures before any positive impact on their repressive behaviour can be felt.

In line with previous research, I expect that, in general, more democratic regimes are less repressive. This relationship is expected to hold true even when the government is faced with dissident activities. Under conditions of internal unrest and protest, the actions of a government in a democratic country are expected to be constrained so that the use of violence by the regime is unlikely. In addition to institutional constraints to violence, democratic regimes can rely on high levels of legitimacy, which makes them less vulnerable to perceiving domestic dissent as a threat to their position in government. This in turn is expected to make democracies less likely to respond with repression to the display of protest (Davenport 1999; Rummel 1997). The following hypothesis can be drawn from this:

H_2: The more democratic a country is, the less repressive is its government.

Some studies have questioned the linear relationship between the degree of democracy and repression. Instead, they have suggested that mixed regimes, meaning those that are neither fully democratic nor fully authoritarian, are more repressive than both democracies and authoritarian regimes (Fein 1995; Hegre *et al.* 2001; Regan and Henderson 2002). Regan and Henderson argue that semi-democracies 'face competing pressures that increase the extent and credibility of the threats they face' (Regan and Henderson 2002: 123). Countries that have adopted some democratic features, such as holding regular elections, while maintaining authoritarian elements – for example, by giving the executive unlimited power and authority – can find themselves in a rather precarious situation. These mixed regimes, or semi-democracies, allow some space for competition and participation, while limiting those rights at the same time. These inconsistencies create tension and dissatisfaction among the population. For example, in Kenya under the single-party regime during the 1960s and 1970s, President Jomo Kenyatta was able to maintain power with comparatively low levels of government coercion, while the multiparty elections under Daniel arap Moi in the 1990s were marred by severe political violence. And, as the events in December 2007 in Kenya have shown, where 250,000 people have been displaced following post-election violence, holding elections in a country where democracy is not fully institutionalized can be a dangerous undertaking. The analysis in the following chapters allows for a non-linear relationship between level of democracy and repression.

As shown in Figure 1.1, the degree of democracy not only has a direct effect on repression but also an indirect one since it can modify a government's reaction to protest and dissent. For example, Davenport (2007a) finds that competition and participation pacify governments when they are faced with violent dissent. Gupta *et al.* (1993) suggest that, in democracies, coercion increases with increasing protest, while in non-democracies the relationship between protest and coercion follows an inverted U-shaped relationship. I therefore hypothesize the following relationship:

> H_3: In democracies, the government is less likely than in authoritarian regimes to use repression in response to dissent.

As indicated above, different types of dissent are likely to trigger different government responses. The government's response, in turn, is expected to be conditioned by the type of political regime within which the interaction between government and opposition takes place. While I expect that more violent forms of protest lead to more violent government responses (see Hypothesis 1.1 above), this linear relationship is likely to be less pronounced in semi-democracies. As explained above, semi-democracies are likely to be particularly susceptible to domestic threats. Therefore, I expect that those regimes that are neither fully democratic nor fully authoritarian react more harshly to peaceful forms of dissent compared to institutionalized democracies or autocracies. Thus:

> H_4: In semi-democracies, governments are more likely to respond with widespread repression to dissent than in democracies or autocracies.

USING DISSENT TO CONFRONT REPRESSION

This section turns around the causal arrow between protest and repression. It looks at the various ways in which state coercion influences protest behaviour. As discussed in the previous chapter, the theoretical arguments and empirical evidence that focus on the impact of repression on dissent cover every possible relationship, including the absence of any relationship. There are four main hypotheses about the relationship between protest and repression that are developed in the literature: (1) positive linear, (2) negative linear, (3) U-relationship and (4) inverted U-relationship (Davis and Ward 1990). Figure 2.1 gives an overview of these hypotheses.

The first scenario hypothesizes that higher levels of repression trigger higher levels of protest. This relationship is generally based on the deprivation approach, which argues that the more repressive the regime is, the more people feel frustrated and react with protest as a result of this frustration (e.g. Lichbach 1987; Opp and Roehl 1990). The hypothesis of a positive linear relationship between repression and protest can also be explained within the framework of rational actors. Within this setting, the relationship between protest and repression is based on responsive and adaptive behaviour, rather than on frustration and regression. If the population is faced with more severe and widespread repression, it will put more effort into limiting the control and power of the state, and rebel against the government. At every level of repression, the opposition attempts to counterbalance the forces of the government, and it does so with similar intensity and force. Therefore, low levels of repression elicit low levels of protest, medium levels of repression produce medium levels of protest, and widespread and violent repression encounters widespread and violent rebellion.

There is also an argument, however, for expecting the opposite relationship, namely that as repression increases, protest decreases. This is shown in the graph in the top right-hand corner of Figure 2.1. This argument is based on the rational theory of deterrence.[4] Adapted to domestic politics, it suggests that as repression increases, protest becomes more costly. The cost-sensitive opposition will therefore react with less dissident activity. *Vice versa*, when negative state sanctions and human rights violations are low, more people are willing to demonstrate and actively protest against the

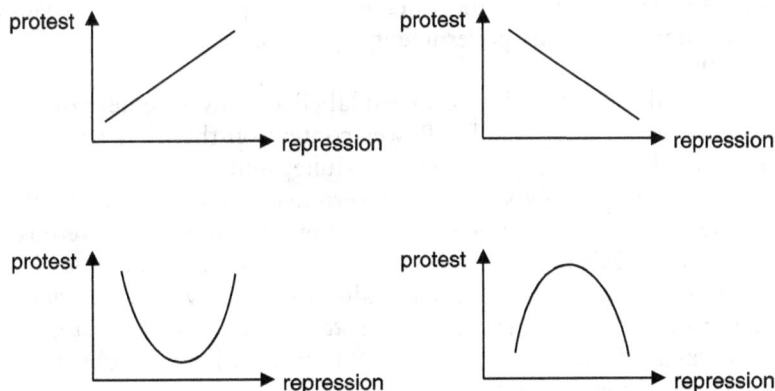

Figure 2.1 Four hypotheses on the impact of repression on protest.

government because open dissent appears to be less risky than under repressive regimes, since the costs of protest are perceived to be lower.

The third relationship, shown in the bottom left-hand corner of Figure 2.1, suggests that both low and high levels of repression lead to high levels of protest, whereas protest is lowest during medium-level repression. This argument is related to the backlash hypothesis. The backlash hypothesis argues that 'harsh coercion accelerates protest' (Francisco 1996: 1182). It argues that extremely severe coercion, while it decreases protest temporarily, increases dissent in the long run, especially when repression is applied indiscriminately (Mason and Krane 1989). The backlash argument is primarily based on a dynamic framework, distinguishing the short-term from the long-term effects of repression on protest. But it also has an important message for the contemporaneous and short-term relationship between protest and repression. It predicts that the population responds with fierce resistance and opposition to very high levels of repression. The reasoning behind this exponential relationship is that very intensive, and then often indiscriminately applied, state repression diminishes the *additional* cost of protest. When governments torture and kill large segments of the population, people might feel they have no choice but to respond with severe resistance. Active opposition may become an obligation. Hence, severe repression is expected to increase levels of protest.

The graph shown in the bottom right-hand corner of Figure 2.1 represents the opposite argument to the one put forward by the backlash hypothesis. The rationale behind the inverted U-hypothesis is that under very repressive regimes, the costs and risks associated with protest and rebellion instil fear in the population and therefore prevent the open display of dissent. On the other hand, under non-repressive regimes, opponents make use of other means of dissent that are available to them to achieve their objectives. For example, they are expected to engage in negotiations with the regime instead of participating in protests and riots. Under semi-repressive regimes, however, protesters can be mobilized, as the level of fear is not prohibitively high, and no other means besides protest seems feasible to voice discontent and resist government repression (Gurr 1970; Muller and Weede 1990).

This inverted U-relationship has been labelled 'power contention theory' or the 'value expectancy' model. Power contention theory is based on the 'rational calculation of expected gain' (Muller and Weede 1994: 40). The opposition will react only when the government seems sufficiently vulnerable and weak so that it is not expected to employ the most severe repression, or merely weak in the sense of not being completely in control of the situation and of the dissidents. The value expectancy model argues that there has to be a real chance for the protest to be successful in order for people to engage in rebellious activity (Rasler 1996). This picks up on the notion of power contention theory and puts it into a wider perspective. The crucial argument of the value expectancy model is that the population will engage in collective dissident action only if they believe that their protest has a real chance of achieving the goal that they are aiming for. Therefore, based on this argument it can be expected that extremely high levels of repression decrease the level of protest.

This discussion highlights that there is no clear picture of what effect repression and the violation of human rights has on protest and dissent. The hypothesis that is tested in the following chapter is based on the argument that the goal of the dissidents is to limit the power of the government or to overthrow the ruling elites. I expect that when faced with government sanctions and coercion, the opposition will initially respond with resistance. In order to stop or limit government repression, the opposition will react with high levels of protest, or an increase in dissident activities. I assume that the opposition will respond with similar levels of intensity. For example, guerrilla warfare as a response to limited government coercion, such as political imprisonment without actually killing large numbers of opponents, would be difficult to mobilize and organize, but would also increase the risk of escalating the violence. Since this would involve very high costs on the side of the opposition, it is not expected to be the most likely strategy. On the other hand, if the opposition responds with confrontational activities that are far less intense than the actions of the government, the success of the resistance would be negligible. Staging a peaceful demonstration in the face of widespread torture and government-sponsored killings would most likely not be perceived as the most promising strategy to end repression, while such severe coercion would probably help to mobilize, and radicalize, parts of the population to join a large-scale and violent resistance. Therefore, I expect a positive relationship between repression and the reaction of the dissidents in the form of protest:

H_5: Repression increases the probability of dissent.

DEMOCRACY AND DISSENT

Just like repression, dissent is likely to be influenced by the political regime in which it operates. For example, in authoritarian regimes, which exclude the majority of the population from participating in the political process, the risk of protest might be particularly high if it is viewed as the only option of voicing discontent with the regime. At the same time, the cost of displaying discontent is also influenced by the characteristics of the political regime.

The concept of the political opportunity structure (Tarrow 1991, 1994) highlights how political regimes can influence domestic protest. Tarrow defines political opportunity structures as a 'consistent – but not necessarily formal, permanent or national – dimension of the political environment which either encourage or discourage people from using collective action' (1994: 18). The political opportunity structure affects the costs, benefits and probability of success of protest movements. It is a function of four elements: (1) the degree of openness or closure of the polity, (2) the stability, or instability, of political alignments, (3) the presence, or absence, of allies and support groups, and (4) the divisions within the elites or its tolerance of protest (Jenkins and Perrow 1977; Tarrow 1991). As the distribution of power changes in the system – for example, through institutional changes – and the authorities become more vulnerable, social movements are more likely to develop.

Tarrow argues that the most significant change in the political opportunity structure results 'from the opening of access to power, from shifts in ruling alignments, from the availability of influential allies and from cleavages within and among elites' (1994: 18). For example, Hipsher (1996) argues that the division in the Chilean government in 1983 led to the rise of the social protest movement. Similarly, in a comparative case study of peasant mobilization in Central America, Brockett (1991) concludes that regime-related factors, such as fragmentation within the ruling elite, as opposed to economic factors, played a substantial role in facilitating peasant mobilization.[5] Analysing the structural factors behind indigenous rebellion in Latin America, Cleary (2000) finds strong support for the argument that the existence of democratic institutions reduces the risk of rebellion:

> In most nondemocratic states, institutional means for the expression of grievance simply do not exist. For minority groups with serious grievances, armed rebellion might be the most effective way to communicate with the regime. But under democratic regimes, there are institutional means for ethnic minorities to express their grievances, such that it is not necessary to resort to the high-cost strategy of rebellion.
>
> (Cleary 2000: 1150)

Focusing on Central America, Booth's (1991) findings also show that regimes that were responsive to peasant grievances managed to avoid rebellion, while those regimes that were the least responsive experienced peasant rebellion. With respect to Africa, Rothchild (1991) argues that regime responsiveness facilitates conflict management and thus reduces the risk of political violence. While these examples from past research focus on rebellion, I argue that those characteristics of democracies that reduce the risk of rebellion also impact upon the non-violent behaviour of regime opponents. In short, domestic conflict in general, and protest in particular, is expected to be influenced by the nature of the political regime, as well as by changes in the institutional structure.

The risk of dissent is expected to decrease the more democratic the political regime is. As the above quote by Cleary (2000) highlights, in democracies institutionalized ways of voicing discontent are accessible to the opposition. At the same time, the nature of a democracy is expected to accommodate opposition grievances before they escalate into large-scale and violent forms of protest. Knowing that one could write to one's elected representative, or simply not vote for a certain candidate, assures citizens certain ways and institutionalized channels for voicing dissent without resorting to demonstrations or even violent forms of protest. Thus:

H_6: The more democratic a country is, the less likely dissent is.

The degree of democracy is also expected to have an indirect effect on dissent by modifying dissidents' behaviour in reaction to state repression. In democracies, citizens enjoy a certain set of rights and protection from the government. When a government steps over the line, the population is likely to protest against the infringement of their human rights and civil liberties. Additionally, due to the democratic institutions and norms, as outlined above, the costs of dissent are expected to be less in democratic than in autocratic regimes. Therefore, I expect that people in democracies are more likely to respond with dissent when their government commits human rights violations than are people in authoritarian regimes. Thus:

H_7: In democracies, the opposition is more likely to respond to repression with protest than in non-democracies.

PROTEST AND REPRESSION: THE IMPACT OF PAST BEHAVIOUR

Protest and repression also have self-perpetuating tendencies. In the case of state coercion, policy inertia reduces the likelihood of radical changes in the government's behaviour. Governments tend to maintain strategies once they have been adopted. Davenport summarizes the argument in the following way: 'previous repression decreases the costs of engaging in this behaviour later because it familiarizes political leaders with what is involved when they employ such behaviour, therefore reducing uncertainty' (2007a: 40). Apart from familiarization and inertia in the executive and administrative apparatus, government agencies, once they have been established, try to justify and perpetuate their existence. When special security forces are put in place to protect the national executive and to control dissident groups, they try to maintain their status and role, and are therefore difficult to dissolve. For example, once Sese Seko Mobutu had installed his civil guard in 1984, the members of the civil guard did not want to lose their position and, as a result, contributed to repressing dissidents simply in order to protect their own interests.

Protest also tends to maintain itself. Once dissidents have successfully organized and carried out protest against the government, they will try to maintain the momentum and sustain the protest. A similar notion is reflected in micromobilization theory and the closely related bandwagon and threshold models. The main argument behind these concepts is that 'small numbers of people trigger the participation of larger numbers of people over time' (Rasler 1996: 134). As discussed earlier, micromobilization theory puts forward the argument that potential rebels can be mobilized for opposition movements by overt dissident behaviour because this shows the willingness and commitment of others. It makes the goal of their activities desirable and raises the social rewards for participating in this movement. The argument of the bandwagon model is based on this rationale. The more people participate in dissident activities, the more likely it is that further people will join them. The threshold model maintains that once a certain, usually unspecified, threshold of number of participants is crossed, the costs of mobilizing a larger crowd are relatively low.[6] Continuing protest is a sign of the willingness and commitment to the collective good of dissent. This encourages further members of the public to participate in the protest activities, as argued in the bandwagon model. It also influences how people perceive the possibility of success of the protest activities. It signals confidence in the desirability of the collective goal and in the prospects of achieving it. Even if further protesters do not join, at least quiet support for the protest within the population might increase. This, in turn, gives the activists more confidence to increase their pressure on the government.

The key elements of the model of repression and the model of dissent have been presented above. In the following, I draw on selected factors that have been found to be of particular importance in the study of repression and dissent to build the theoretical models that are put to empirical tests in the following chapter.

MODEL OF REPRESSION

Dissent has consistently been found to increase repression (e.g. Davenport 2007a; Regan and Henderson 2002). When a sufficiently large number of people become so disillusioned with the government that they take action and protest, the government takes drastic measures to extinguish those threats to its authority. But not all dissent activities are equally threatening to the government, and therefore not all dissent activities elicit the same response from the state. Governments are likely to categorize dissent activities along two dimensions: first, whether the event is violent and, second, whether it is an isolated event or whether the activity can be assumed to be part of a wider campaign against the government (Carey 2009). Violent dissent poses a particularly significant threat to the government and is therefore particularly likely to trigger a violent and excessive response from the state, as the government will be determined to end this kind of protest quickly and effectively.

At the same time, it is unlikely that governments employ the same kind of response to small-scale versus large-scale violent attacks. In order to empirically investigate whether small-scale and large-scale violent dissent leads to different responses by the government, I distinguish between three different types of dissent: peaceful dissent (in the form of peaceful anti-government demonstrations and strikes), small-scale violent dissent (in the form of violent riots) and large-scale violent dissent (in the form of guerrilla warfare and rebellion). Large-scale violent dissent is expected to have the most substantial impact on government coercion, and peaceful dissent is expected to make only a small difference to the level of state repression. To test for the impact of political regimes on repression, I include a measure for democracy and a squared term of the democracy scale in the model of repression.

Additional control variables are included in the model. Political instability – for example, in the form of regime change – is often associated with increased domestic conflict (Davenport 1999; Hegre *et al.* 2001; Tarrow 1994; Zanger 2000). States tend to use repression when they are faced with threats in the form of protest and rebellion. Political instability poses similar threats. In order to analyse how governments react to dissent, it is necessary to take into account the constraints under which states operate. I expect that political instability is particularly destabilizing and threatening to a government, hence resulting in higher levels of repression during such times.

One of the most consistent findings in research on severe human rights violations has been the link between civil war and state coercion (e.g. Davenport 2007a; McCormick and Mitchell 1997; Poe *et al.* 1999; Zanger 2000). A civil war poses a major threat to a government and indicates high levels of political instability, hence making it very likely that extreme measures in the form of widespread repression are used to end such conflict. The extreme and violent circumstances of a civil war can also be used by governments to justify the use of repression to restore law and order, by whatever means necessary. Therefore, I expect that repression increases during times of civil war.[7]

Two additional variables have become part of the core set of indicators that are used to explain human rights abuses: economic development and population size (e.g. Davenport 2007a; Henderson 1991; Mitchell and McCormick 1988; Poe *et al.* 1999). Large populations place a particular stress on natural resources and as such on governments, therefore making them more susceptible to potential or real threats. When governments are more likely to perceive certain groups or behaviours as threatening, they are more likely to employ repression to counter this threat (Henderson 1993; Poe 2004; Poe and Tate 1994). With respect to economic development, Mitchell and McCormick argue that '[t]he poorest countries, with substantial social and political tensions created by economic scarcity, would be most unstable and thus most apt to use repression in order to maintain control' (1988: 478). Additionally, people in richer countries are expected to be more satisfied, and are therefore expected to be less likely to challenge the government than people in poorer countries, which would increase the risk of repression under such poorer economic conditions (Henderson 1991). In my model of repression, I control only for population size but not for economic development due to the nature of my sample, as it focuses mostly on developing countries. Differences in poverty levels are picked up by regional differences between Africa and Latin America.[8] To account for differences between sub-Saharan Africa and Latin America, I include a dummy variable that captures all African countries. This variable also accounts for the substantially higher levels of repression in Latin America compared to Africa, particularly during the 1980s. To summarize, the probability of repression is explained as a function of the following variables:

Pr(Repression) = f(Repression$_{t-1}$, Peaceful Dissent, Small-Scale Violent Dissent, Large-Scale Violent Dissent, Democracy, Democracy^2, Political Instability, Civil War, Population Size, Africa Dummy)

MODEL OF DISSENT

This section turns the causal arrow around and analyses variations in dissent. As with repression, dissent has high start-up costs and, once these are overcome, protest activities are likely to continue. Therefore, as in the model of repression, I include a lagged dependent variable in the analysis. The core variable of interest in this model is the degree of repression that is employed by the government. The literature that investigates the impact of repression on dissent is characterized by opposing theoretical arguments and empirical findings. In the model of dissent, I include indicators for different levels of repression, to test their impact on the behaviour of the opposition. To capture the impact of the political regime, I control for the degree of democracy, as well as for squared democracy, to allow for a non-linear relationship between democracy and dissent.

Consistent with the arguments about changes in the political opportunity structure outlined earlier, I expect that regime instability in the form of changes to the political system are expected to increase the risk of dissent. Changes to the rules of political behaviour and interaction create a volatile situation, which is likely to be exploited by the opposition by staging protest activities (Fearon and Laitin 2003).

As already mentioned in relation to the model of repression, civil war is an extreme form of instability and as such is expected to have a similar effect to that of political instability on the probability of dissent. During a civil war, governments are particularly vulnerable, while the fact that the country is engulfed in a civil war might facilitate the mobilization of protest activities against the government. Therefore, I include a measure for civil war in the model of dissent, expecting that dissent increases during times of civil war.[9] Similar to the model of repression, population size is expected to increase the probability of dissent, but for different reasons. Countries with larger populations provide a larger pool of potential protesters, making it more likely to overcome the problem of collective action. Additionally, larger populations can make it more difficult for governments to solve intrastate political problems, therefore increasing the risk of dissent (Herbst 2000).[10] Finally, I include again a dummy variable for African countries to account for the systematic differences between Africa and Latin America. The model analysing the probability of dissent is summarized below:[11]

$$Pr(\text{Dissent}) = f(\text{Dissent}_{t-1}, \text{Repression}, \text{Democracy}, \text{Democracy}^2, \text{Political Instability}, \text{Civil War}, \text{Population Size}, \text{Africa Dummy})$$

SUMMARY

This chapter has established the meanings of protest and repression as they are understood in the context of this book. It developed two separate models, one to explain how protest and democracy influence repression and one to investigate how repression and democracy influence dissent. Various, and often contradicting, theories and empirical findings have been put forward in the literature. I have argued in this chapter that the conflictual behaviour of one actor leads to the conflictual behaviour of the other actor, expecting that repression follows dissent, and equally that dissent follows repression. If the political regime is characterized by democratic institutions, which emphasize compromise and peaceful solutions of conflict, then those democratic institutions are expected to lower the risk of violent behaviour on both sides: the government and the opposition. The following chapter turns to the operationalization of the concepts discussed above, and empirically tests the models of repression and dissent.

Notes

1 While the empirical analysis in Chapter 3 focuses exclusively on 'open physical confrontations', Chapter 4 extends the concept of political conflict to include non-physical struggle as well, widening the spectrum of political conflict that is analysed to range from negative statements, verbal threats and deadlock in negotiations to full-fledged guerrilla warfare and rebellion. This is discussed more fully in Chapter 4.

2 Other studies have broken the two general groups – state and opposition – into more specific categories, such as reformers, military and opposition (Zielinski 1999) or the government, rebels and the mob (Ginkel and Smith 1999), for example.

3 For excellent analyses of in-group dynamics, see, for example, Kalyvas (2006) and Weinstein (2007).

4 Deterrence theory has originally been developed in International Relations theory in order to explain military policies during the Cold War (George and Smoke 1974). 'A rational theory of deterrence focuses on the policies and capabilities a defender can utilize to persuade an attacker not to initiate some specified

action. . . . Deterrence is predicted to succeed when the expected utility of using force is less than the expected utility of not using force' (Huth and Russett 1990: 469).

5 He also points out that the perception of threat in the form of social movements and protest often caused the elite to unify and overcome any differences, resulting in state repression and intimidation.

6 Since I do not look at the specific number of dissidents involved in protest activities, I do not strictly apply the concepts of micromobilization theory and the bandwagon model, but these models nevertheless highlight the point made above, namely that protest is likely to persist for some time.

7 Several studies argue that when a government is involved in an international war, the threat perception, and with it the risk of repression, increases (Krain 1997; Poe and Tate 1994; Tarrow 1994). Due to the small number of cases of international war involvement in the sample, I do not include this variable in the analyses presented in this book. When I included international war in robustness tests, this indicator was not statistically significant.

8 I have tested the impact of economic development by including a measure for GNP per capita in the analysis of repression, but this variable is far from reaching any meaningful levels of statistical significance. This is not uncommon for such a sample, as previous studies that have focused on developing countries also found no support for the economic development argument, most likely due to the limited variance of this variable in such a setting (Harrelson-Stephens and Callaway 2003; Richards *et al.* 2001).

9 Although rebellion and civil war are sometimes used synonymously, they describe two conceptually different phenomena. First, civil war requires both a government and a non-government actor to be involved in the activities and, second, in order to qualify as civil war, the threshold of 25 battle-related deaths per year needs to be crossed (see also Carey 2007). The descriptive statistics also show that the measurement of large-scale violent dissent and civil war picks up different, although related, activities. The correlation between the two variables is 0.548 and the variance inflation factor is 1.43.

10 Like repression, dissent has also often been argued to be influenced by the level of economic development. Oberschall argues that '[t]he central concern of conflict theory becomes mobilization, organization, and collective action. Grievances, discontent, and societal breakdown are not ignored insofar as they will affect the resource base of the various parties and their mobilizations, organizations and collective action costs' (1993: 55). Therefore, it could be argued that higher economic development results in better resources for the opposition and hence increases the level of dissent. On the other hand, one might expect that people in poorer countries have less to lose and are therefore more likely to take their discontent to the streets. Additionally, economic development can be seen as an indicator of the state's strength, arguing that weaker countries are more likely to experience dissent (Fearon and Laitin 2003). However, as indicated above, the variable for economic development does not add any explanatory power in this setting, most likely due to the limited variation of economic development within the sample of African and Latin American countries, particularly in the presence of the dummy variable for Africa. It is also reasonable to assume that not just population size, but also the concentration of the population influences dissent. In a robustness test, I included population density, but this variable did not have a measurable impact upon dissent. In the interest of parsimony, I excluded population density from the models presented and discussed in the book.

11 There is a growing literature that contrasts greed- versus grievances-motivated rebellions, and investigates the feasibility of rebellion (e.g. Collier 2000; Collier and Hoeffler 2004; Fearon and Laitin 2003). But since many of the prominent

indicators in this work have received mixed empirical support, such as the impact of rough terrain, oil dependence, neighbouring rebellions and ethnic heterogeneity (e.g. Carey 2007), and because these factors relate to only one particular type of dissent, I do not include them in my model of dissent. I have included measures for ethnic heterogeneity, oil dependence and rough terrain in alternative specifications of the model, but these variables were not statistically significant.

3 A macro-level analysis

After presenting the theoretical framework, this chapter provides a general, macro-level analysis of how protest and political regimes impact upon repression, and of how political regimes and repression affect protest. It focuses on Latin America and sub-Saharan Africa from 1977 to 2002. Quantitative studies have traditionally used samples that pooled the largest number of countries for which data were available (e.g. Davenport 1995; Muller and Weede 1994; Poe et al. 1999). But the relationship between the variables of interest might substantially differ, and be driven by completely different processes, in a sample of widely diverse countries. In this book, I follow the approach of restricting my analysis to a set of more homogeneous cases.[1] I concentrate my analysis on a relatively similar set of countries from Latin America and sub-Saharan Africa. Although each country has its own unique history and features, the Latin American countries share many characteristics, such as history, culture and societal qualities, which influence the relationship between dissent and state repression. Also African countries share many characteristics that are not controlled for in the analysis.[2] In the following, I first discuss the operationalization of the variables. Then I outline the methodology that is employed to analyse the data, before presenting the results of the investigation of protest and repression in Latin America and Africa.

MEASUREMENT

Government repression can express itself in various forms. I focus on violations of security rights, or life integrity rights, such as the use of torture, political imprisonment, extrajudicial killings and disappearances. To operationalize such forms of human rights violations, or repression, I use the Political Terror Scale (PTS), which is the most widely used indicator of this concept in the quantitative literature.[3] This standard-based measure is based on categories developed by Gastil (1980) and was originally created by Stohl, Gibney and colleagues (Gibney and Dalton 1996; Poe and Tate 1994; Stohl and Carleton 1985). Amnesty International Human Rights reports and US State Department Country Reports are used to assign countries to categories according to their respect for life integrity rights. The contents of these two sets of reports are analysed and a value from one to five is assigned to each country for each year, according to where it fits on the scale shown in Table 3.1.

For the analysis I use the data based on the Amnesty International reports. For the years in which these reports were not issued, I take the scores from the US State Department Country Reports. This is the procedure commonly applied in such instances. In comparison to the Amnesty International reports, the State Department used to be slightly biased against leftist countries, where they tended to treat their allies and trading partners less harshly in their human rights reports than Amnesty International does. However, the differences between the two sets of reports have decreased over time (Poe *et al.* 2001).

Table 3.2 shows the distribution of the Political Terror Scale for the complete sample and for the two sub-groups, Latin America and sub-Saharan Africa, from 1976 to 2002. Level 2 (limited political imprisonment, with torture and political murder being rare) and Level 3 (extensive political imprisonment, torture and political murder being more common) are the

Table 3.1 The Political Terror Scale (PTS)

Level	Description	Examples
1	Countries under secure rule of law, people are not imprisoned for their view, and torture is rare or exceptional. Political murders are extremely rare.	Botswana during 1980s and 1990s, Costa Rica during most years between 1976 and 2003
2	There is a limited amount of imprisonment for non-violent political activity. However, few persons are affected, torture and beatings are exceptional. Political murder is rare.	Bolivia during the mid-1980s, Benin and Gabon during most years between 1976 and 2003
3	There is extensive political imprisonment, or a recent history of such imprisonment. Execution or other political murders and brutality may be common. Unlimited detention, with or without a trial, for political views is accepted.	Sudan from 1977–86, Nicaragua during the 1990s
4	Civil and political rights violations have expanded to large numbers of the population. Murders, disappearances and torture are a common part of life. In spite of its generality, on this level terror affects those who interest themselves in politics or ideas.	Uganda and Somalia since the mid-1990s, El Salvador and Guatemala during the early 1990s
5	Terror has expanded to the whole population. The leaders of these societies place no limits on the means or thoroughness with which they pursue personal or ideological goals.	Argentina during the late 1970s, Rwanda between 1994 and 1999

Source: The Political Terror Scale (PTS), at http://www.politicalterrorscale.org/

Table 3.2 Distribution of the Political Terror Scale

Level	All countries %	Latin America %	Sub-Saharan Africa %
1	8.07	9.35	7.34
2	34.74	26.94	39.17
3	30.58	33.39	28.99
4	18.13	20.48	16.79
5	8.48	9.84	7.71
Total	100.00	100.00	100.00

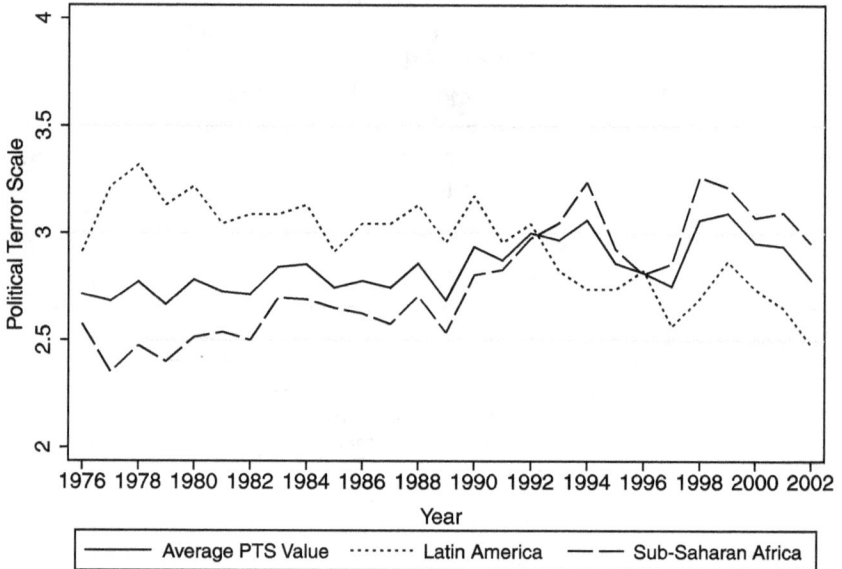

Figure 3.1 Average values of Political Terror Scale across time.

most common levels of life integrity violations. More widespread repression, which affects large parts of the population, as well as the absence of repression, are less common. The table shows that, between 1976 and 2002, Latin American governments were more repressive than their African counterparts. For Africa, 54 per cent of the observations fall into category three or higher, whereas for Latin America the corresponding figure is 63 per cent. The dummy variable that captures all African countries in the sample accounts for these different levels of repression in the two regions.

Figure 3.1 shows how the average level of repression has changed over time, both for all countries and for the two regions separately. The overall average shows a small, but not continuous, upward trend. Over time, human rights record have improved in Latin America, while the human rights situation has deteriorated in Africa.

The data measuring dissent are taken from the Cross-National Time-Series (CNTS) Data Archive.[4] These data count how often domestic conflict events have occurred in a year, using the *New York Times* as the source of information. The dissent variable that I use in my analysis is based on the following five indicators.

1   *Anti-government demonstrations:* Any peaceful public gathering of at least 100 people for the primary purpose of displaying or voicing their opposition to government policies or authority, excluding demonstrations of a distinctly anti-foreign nature.
2   *General strikes:* Any strike of 1,000 or more industrial or service workers that involves more than one employer and that is aimed at national government policies or authority.
3   *Riots:* Any violent demonstration or clash of more than 100 citizens involving the use of physical force.
4   *Guerrilla warfare:* Any armed activity, sabotage, or bombings carried on by independent bands of citizens or irregular forces and aimed at the overthrow of the present regime.
5   *Revolutions:* Any illegal or forced change in the top government elite, any attempt at such a change, or any successful or unsuccessful armed rebellion whose aim is independence from the central government.

(Banks 2008: 11–12)

These five variables measure various dissent activities, ranging from peaceful activities and low-intensity dissent to large-scale violent revolution. On the basis of these variables, I create an ordinal scale that captures the three main categories of dissent activities that I have outlined in Chapter 2: peaceful dissent, small-scale violent dissent and large-scale violent dissent, or rebellion. To arrive at this categorization, I first change the count variables into binary variables, coding years in which a specified event occurred at least once as one, and all other years as zero. Despite the loss of information, this procedure generates a useful measure for three reasons. First, the loss of information is relatively small since most dissent activities are coded as occurring only once during any one particular year. Second, the highest costs for the opposition to overcome in order to show dissent are those that are attached to the first activity. After this, the marginal costs decline. Therefore, the question *whether* to undertake an activity or not, is arguably more important than the question of *how many times* an activity has been undertaken.[5]

In a second step, I aggregate the original five variables into three groups, depending on the nature of the protest activity. Anti-government demonstrations and general strikes capture peaceful forms of protest. Therefore, both of these variables are used to code peaceful dissent. Riots are also aimed at voicing opposition to government policies or authority, but are violent. In contrast to guerrilla warfare and revolutions, however, their aim is more limited and they generally occur on a smaller scale. I use the original riots variable to operationalize small-scale violent dissent. Guerrilla warfare and revolutions measure violent dissent activities that are aimed at over-throwing the government. I utilize both variables to operationalize large-scale violent dissent.[6] The last step to create my dissent variable uses these three binary measures to form an ordinal scale, ranging from no dissent (value zero) to large-scale violent dissent (value three), where each observation measures the most severe form of dissent that occurs during that particular year in that particular country. The distribution of this new ordinal dissent variable is shown in Table 3.3.

Just over half the sample is coded as no dissent occurring, while almost 30 per cent of cases are coded as experiencing large-scale violent dissent in the form of guerrilla warfare or rebellion. Peaceful protest and small-scale violent dissent occur about equally frequently in the whole sample. But there are interesting differences when we look at the two regions separately. During the observed time period, African countries experienced no dissent most of the time, but in almost 30 per cent of observations large-scale violent dissent was recorded. Peaceful dissent, on the other hand, was very rare. In contrast to this, Latin America experienced dissent far more frequently, with only 39 per cent of observations coded as any dissent being absent. But peaceful dissent occurred almost as frequently as large-scale violent dissent. This shows that while opposition in Africa was less likely to protest against the government, when they did, they did so with an organized, violent and large-scale campaign. In Latin America, people took to the streets for less severe and intense protest activities more often than in Africa.

To measure democracy, I employ the widely used 21-point Polity scale (Marshall and Jaggers 2002), which I have normalized to range from zero (full autocracy) to 20 (full democracy). To capture political instability, I use a dichotomous measure by Fearon and Laitin (2003), which indicates changes of more than two points on the polity variable over the past three years. Civil war is measured with the UCDP/PRIO Armed Conflict Dataset, version 4-2007 (Gleditsch *et al.* 2002). The binary variable is coded one for all country years in which a civil war occurred, zero otherwise. Civil war is defined as 'a contested incompatibility that concerns government and/or

Table 3.3 Distribution of dissent

Level	Label	All countries	Latin America	Sub-Saharan Africa
0	No dissent	53.47	38.81	61.50
1	Peaceful dissent	9.97	21.58	3.61
2	Small-scale violent dissent	9.34	14.33	6.61
3	Large-scale violent dissent	27.22	25.28	28.28
Total		100.00	100.00	100.00

Note: The figures represent percentages

territory where the use of armed force between two parties, of which at least one is the government of a state, results in at least 25 battle-related deaths' (Harbom *et al.* 2007: 3).[7] Finally, population size is taken from the World Bank World Development Indicators.

ANALYSING REPRESSION AND DISSENT

To empirically investigate the models presented above, I use ordered probit analysis with robust standard errors. These models, introduced to the social sciences by McKelvey and Zavoina (1975), are based on a measurement model in which a latent variable is mapped onto an observed variable. The observed variable, such as the ordinal repression or dissent variables, is considered as providing incomplete information about the underlying variable. As a result, the thresholds of change, or cut points τ, are also parameters to be estimated along with the coefficients of the explanatory variables.[8]

Because both dissent and repression are ordered variables, I convert the two ordered scales into a set of binary variables when used on the right-hand side of the equation. In the model of repression, I use dummy variables for the individual levels of the Political Terror Scale lagged by one year as additional explanatory variables. The binary variable of PTS Level 1 is used as control group. Similarly, the ordered dissent variable, ranging from zero (no dissent) to three (large-scale violent dissent), is divided into three separate dummy variables for each type of dissent. The absence of dissent is used as the reference category. In both models, the lagged dependent variable is included for theoretical reasons, as discussed in the previous chapter, but also for methodological reasons, to account for autocorrelation. The following section discusses the results of the model of repression, before moving on to the results of the model of dissent.

The impact of dissent and political regimes on repression

The results of the ordered probit analysis of repression are shown in Table 3.4.[9]

First, I briefly discuss the results of the control variables before presenting how dissent and regime type impact upon repression. All control variables are statistically significant and, with the sign in the hypothesized direction, confirm past research in these areas. Political instability and civil war increase the risk of repression, while more populous countries are also more likely to suffer from state coercion. The dummy variable for Africa reflects the distribution of the Political Terror Scale shown in Table 3.2, indicating that during the period 1977–2002, governments in Latin America were more repressive than their counterparts in Africa.

To get a better idea of how some of these variables influence repression, Table 3.5 presents the changes in the predicted probabilities of the Political

Table 3.4 Results of the ordered probit model for repression

	Coefficient	Robust std err.
PTS Level 2_{t-1}	0.949***	0.135
PTS Level 3_{t-1}	1.683***	0.148
PTS Level 4_{t-1}	2.719***	0.173
PTS Level 5_{t-1}	3.628***	0.218
Peaceful dissent	0.101	0.103
Small-scale violent dissent	0.320**	0.105
Large-scale violent dissent	0.365***	0.087
Democracy	0.040	0.026
Democracy^2	−0.004**	0.001
Political instability	0.183*	0.083
Civil war	0.889***	0.103
Population size^a	0.201***	0.025
Africa	−0.362***	0.076
τ_1	2.376	0.392
τ_2	4.353	0.403
τ_3	5.930	0.409
τ_4	7.454	0.424
Log pseudolikelihood	−1520.174	
χ^2	924.16***	
Pseudo R^2	34.84	
N	1615	

a Variable log-transformed due to skewed distribution.
* $p < 0.05$, ** $p < 0.01$, *** $p < 0.001$, two-tailed tests.

Terror Scale under various scenarios for Latin America and Africa. The first row for each region shows the predicted probability of each PTS level in an average country.[10] The subsequent rows indicate how the predicted probabilities of each level of the PTS change when the corresponding independent variable, shown in the first column, changes from zero to one. Finally, the last column in Table 3.5 shows the average of the absolute values of the changes across all five categories of the PTS scale.

The baseline probabilities in the top row show that a country in Latin America had a 0.523 probability of experiencing extensive political imprisonment and some political murders and brutality (PTS Level 3). At the same time, there was a 0.103 probability of widespread murders, disappearances and torture (PTS Level 4). The equivalent figure for Africa is about half that size at 0.053, while situations where those life integrity rights are respected (PTS Level 1) were twice as likely in Africa than in Latin America. In short, the baseline model shows again that life integrity rights were at higher risk in Latin America compared to Africa.

The average change presented in the last column in Table 3.5 provides us with a picture of how past repression, instability of the political regime and civil war affect repression on average. First, note that these variables affect

Table 3.5 Changes in predicted probabilities of repression

	PTS Level 1	PTS Level 2	PTS Level 3	PTS Level 4	PTS Level 5	Average change
Latin America						
Baseline[a]	0.011	0.361	0.523	0.103	0.003	
PTS Level 2$_{t-1}$	−0.016	−0.291	0.070	0.217	0.020	0.123
PTS Level 3$_{t-1}$	−0.027	−0.442	−0.001	0.400	0.070	0.188
PTS Level 4$_{t-1}$	−0.025	−0.478	−0.312	0.470	0.345	0.326
PTS Level 5$_{t-1}$	−0.016	−0.420	−0.472	0.157	0.752	0.363
Political instability	−0.003	−0.060	0.019	0.041	0.003	0.025
Civil war	−0.007	−0.226	−0.046	0.243	0.036	0.112
Africa						
Baseline[a]	0.026	0.448	0.433	0.053	0.001	
PTS Level 2$_{t-1}$	−0.036	−0.318	0.194	0.153	0.008	0.142
PTS Level 3$_{t-1}$	−0.058	−0.500	0.202	0.323	0.033	0.142
PTS Level 4$_{t-1}$	−0.055	−0.582	−0.115	0.529	0.224	0.301
PTS Level 5$_{t-1}$	−0.038	−0.542	−0.350	0.304	0.626	0.372
Political instability	−0.007	−0.065	0.043	0.027	0.001	0.029
Civil war	−0.017	−0.281	0.089	0.193	0.016	0.119

a The baseline does not represent changes in the predicted probabilities but the predicted probabilities of the baseline models. For this calculation, political instability and civil war were set at zero, all other variables at their mean.

Note: The figures in the last column, 'Average change', represent the average of the absolute values of the changes across all five categories of the PTS scale.

repression to very similar degrees in Africa and in Latin America. Second, PTS Levels 4 and 5 at time t-1 have, on average, the largest impact on PTS levels at time t. The picture that presents itself from these results shows that past levels of repression are either maintained or intensified. Looking at the changes in the predicted probabilities if violations at PTS Level 2 occur at time t-1, we can see that this actually decreases the probability of the same level of repression in the following year (by −0.291 for Latin America and by −0.318 for Africa). But the occurrence of PTS Level 2 at time t-1 increases the probability of more severe forms of state coercion, which is shown by the positive figures for both regions. This suggests that once governments make concessions to the respect for life integrity rights, they find themselves on the slippery slope towards using even more repression. And, once severe repression occurs, the probability of similar levels of repression happening in the following year increases substantially. For example, repression at PTS Level 5 at time t-1 increases the probability of PTS Level 5 at time t by 0.752 in Latin America and by 0.626 in Africa. If added to the baseline probability, this most severe form of repression becomes the most likely outcome, despite this level of coercion being normally a very rare event. This highlights how important it is to prevent the outbreak of repression in the first place, including coercion that happens initially only on a limited scale.

Table 3.5 also shows that civil war has a much larger effect on repression than political instability. While the instability of political institutions is seen as threatening by governments, and increases the risk of repression, civil wars generally represent far greater challenges to government authority. Additionally, during civil wars, governments can often identify certain groups as the main threat, and therefore target their followers and sympathizers.

The results shown in Table 3.4 support the general hypothesis that dissent increases the probability of repression (H$_1$). But only two of the three dissent indicators are statistically significant. Only violent forms of dissent increase the probability of state coercion, while peaceful protest in the form of strikes and anti-government demonstrations fails to impact upon repression. To show the impact of the three different types of dissent on repression, I calculate the changes that occur in the predicted probabilities for the five PTS levels when a particular form of dissent takes place. Figures 3.2 and 3.3 show the changes in the predicted probabilities for Latin America and Africa. The first group of bars indicates how the predicted probabilities of repression change when peaceful dissent occurs (compared to no dissent taking place). Each individual bar shows the changes in the five levels of the Political Terror Scale. The second group of bars shows the changes in the predicted probabilities when riots occur, and the last one when large-scale violent dissent in the form of guerrilla warfare or rebellion takes place. The (very small) solid black bars show the predicted probabilities of PTS Level 1 change, the striped bars refer to PTS Level 2, the dotted bars represent the changes in the predicted probabilities of PTS Level 3, the cross-checked bars refer to changes in PTS Level 4 and the solid white ones to PTS Level 5.

The graphs show that any type of dissent makes more severe and

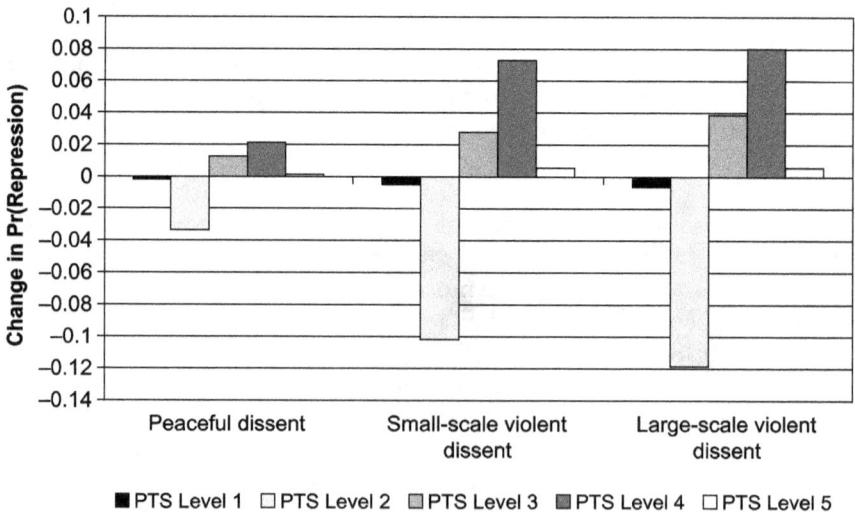

Figure 3.2 Change in predicted probabilities of repression in Latin America.

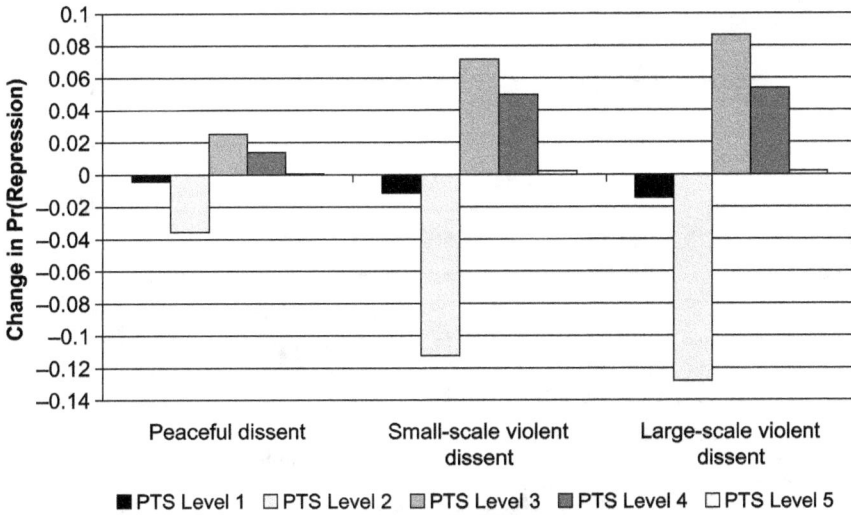

Figure 3.3 Change in predicted probabilities of repression in Africa.

widespread violations of life integrity rights more likely and the respect for such rights less likely. The two figures also show that Latin American governments are more likely to respond more harshly to dissent than are African rulers. When any form of dissent occurs, extensive political imprisonment and some political murders and police brutality (PTS Level 3) see the largest increase in probability in Africa, whereas in Latin America, widespread murders, disappearances and torture (PTS Level 4) show the largest increase in predicted probabilities under such threats. Figure 3.2 also supports the argument that the greater the threat is, the more likely more severe repression becomes. This shows that violent forms of dissent lead to more repressive government reaction than non-violent forms of dissent, supporting Hypothesis 1.1. Peaceful dissent leads to only small changes in the predicted probabilities of repression, in addition to not reaching conventional levels of statistical significance.

In absolute terms, repression at PTS Level 3 is the most likely form of response to any dissent in both regions. Figures 3.4 and 3.5 plot the predicted probabilities of repression under each possible scenario of dissent (no dissent, peaceful dissent, small-scale violent dissent, large-scale violent dissent) for Africa and Latin America. Comparing the two figures shows that PTS Level 3 is always the most common extent of coercion in Latin America, even in the absence of any dissent activities. In Africa, however, PTS Level 2, meaning very limited coercion, is the most common form of repression when the government is not threatened by any dissident activities. When peaceful dissent occurs, there is a 54 per cent risk of extensive political imprisonment

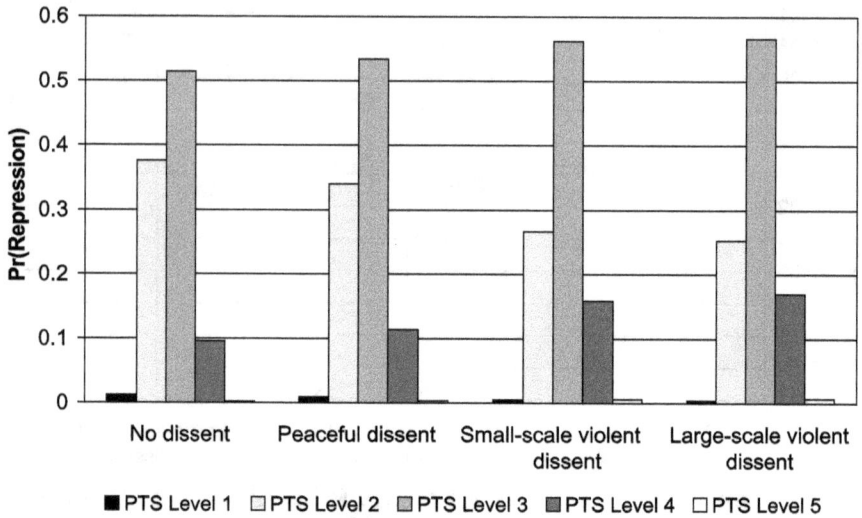

Figure 3.4 Predicted probabilities of repression in Latin America.

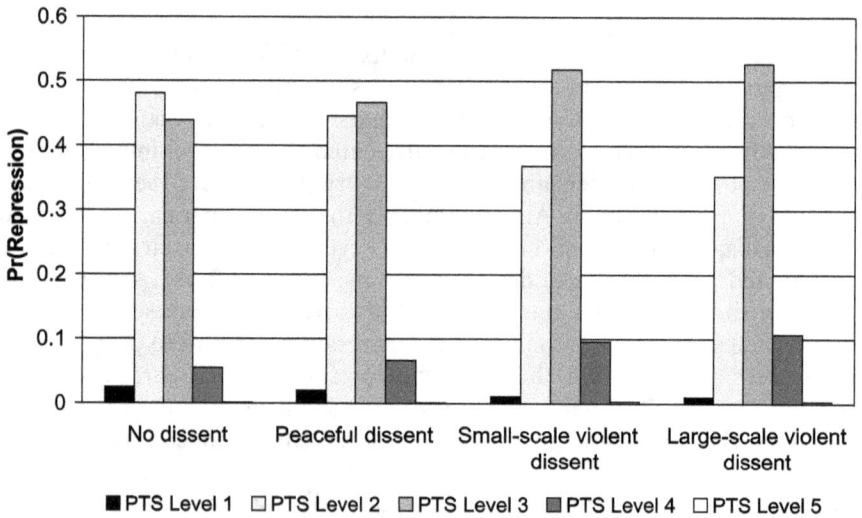

Figure 3.5 Predicted probabilities of repression in Africa.

and some political murders and brutality (PTS Level 3) in Latin America, whereas the comparable risk in Africa is only 46 per cent.

In the following I discuss the influence of regime type on repression. The results presented in Table 3.4 suggest that the most democratic regimes are less repressive, as the coefficient of the squared democracy scale is statistically significant and negative. The democracy scale is positive, which would indicate an inverted U-shaped relationship between democracy and repression, but the coefficient is not statistically significant. Figures 3.6 and 3.7 show how the predicted probabilities for PTS Levels 1 to 4 change across regime types, ranging from full autocracies (Democracy level 0) to full democracies (Democracy level 20).[11] PTS Level 5 is not included as its predicted probabilities are very close to zero across the whole range of regime type.

There are several things worth pointing out in Figures 3.6 and 3.7. First, they show that the relationship between regime type and repression does not take on a linear form, therefore providing qualified support for H2, which argued that the more democratic a country, the less repressive is its government. While democracies are indeed the least repressive countries, not every step towards a more fully institutionalized democracy proportionally decreases the risk of repression. Instead, the predicted probabilities of PTS Levels 2 and 4 hint at an (inverted) U-shaped relationship. Widespread murders, disappearances and torture (PTS Level 4) are slightly less likely to occur in the most authoritarian regimes compared to authoritarian regimes that have some democratic features. But for regimes that are above the bottom third of the democracy scale, the risk of severe repression (PTS Level 4) decreases steadily (although this is less pronounced for Africa than for Latin America). At the same time, the risk of very limited violations (PTS Level 2) increases steadily, and quite substantially so. Figure 3.6 shows that in a complete autocracy in Latin America, there is a 27 per cent chance of only very limited violations (PTS Level 2), which drops to 24 per cent in a country

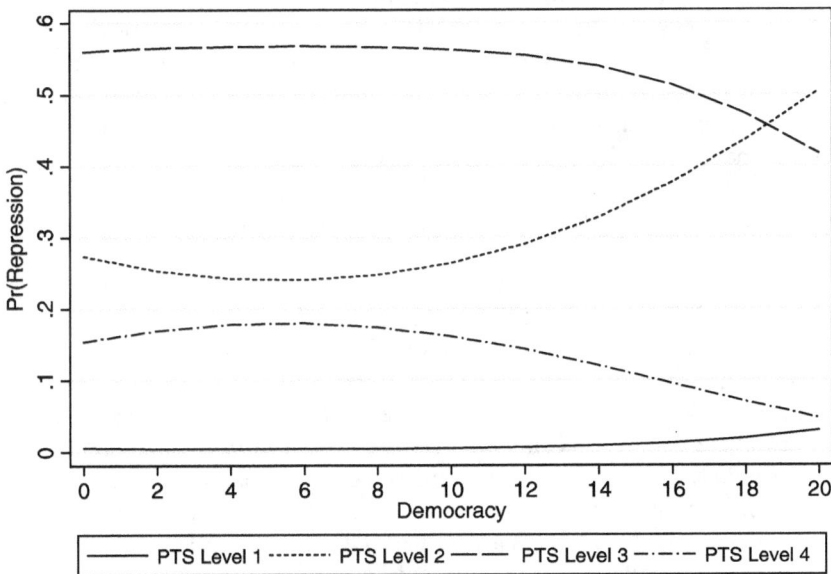

Figure 3.6 Predicted probabilities of repression under different levels of democracy, Latin America.

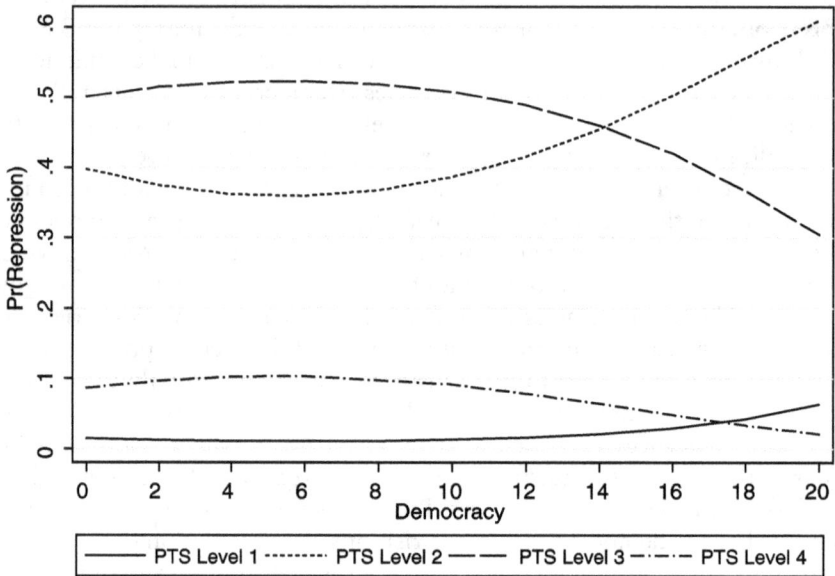

Figure 3.7 Predicted probabilities of repression under different levels of democracy, sub-Saharan Africa.

at point five of this democracy scale, but just touches on 51 per cent in a fully established democracy. This means that while in almost all regime types, limited life integrity violations, represented by PTS Level 3, are by far the most likely scenario, with a probability of up to 0.57, violations on PTS Level 2 take over as the most common form of repression for the regimes that are placed in the top two categories of the democracy scale. This is similar to the findings of Davenport and Armstrong (2004), which suggest that only in regimes that are in the top three democracy categories is there a negative relationship between degree of democracy and repression, while they find no relationship below this threshold. The initially rather flat curve of the predicted probabilities of PTS Level 3 further supports this argument.

This picture is slightly different for Africa. Similar to Latin America, repression at PTS Level 3 is the most common degree of repression in most regimes. But the gap to the probability of PTS Level 2 is far smaller in Africa than in Latin America. Probably more importantly, for African countries, PTS Level 2 takes over as the most likely extent of state coercion sooner than for Latin American ones. Countries in the top quarter of the democracy scale are more likely to experience only limited coercion than any other degree of repression. Finally, it is interesting to note that while the predicted probability of no repression lingers around zero for most regimes, it increases for the most democratic countries, but does so earlier in Africa than in Latin America. Adding this element to the overall picture, this suggests that, in Latin America, the pacifying effect of democracy on governments takes places only in the most democratic countries. In Africa, however, this effect can be felt in countries that are in the top quarter of the democracy scale.

So far, I have evaluated the impact of different types of dissent and regime type on repression independently of one another. But, as put forward in the previous chapter, democracy is also expected to dampen a government's response when faced with dissent.

Figures 3.8 to 3.11 compare the predicted probabilities of repression

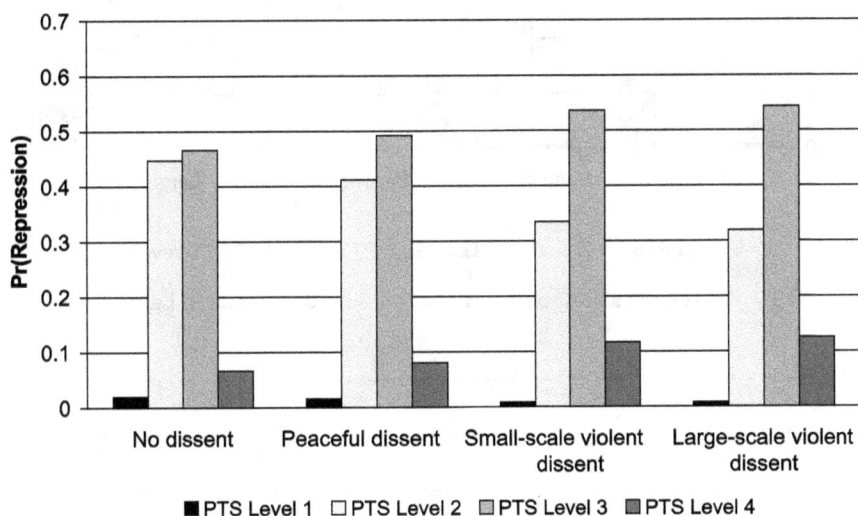

Figure 3.8 Repression as response to dissent in non-democracies, Africa.

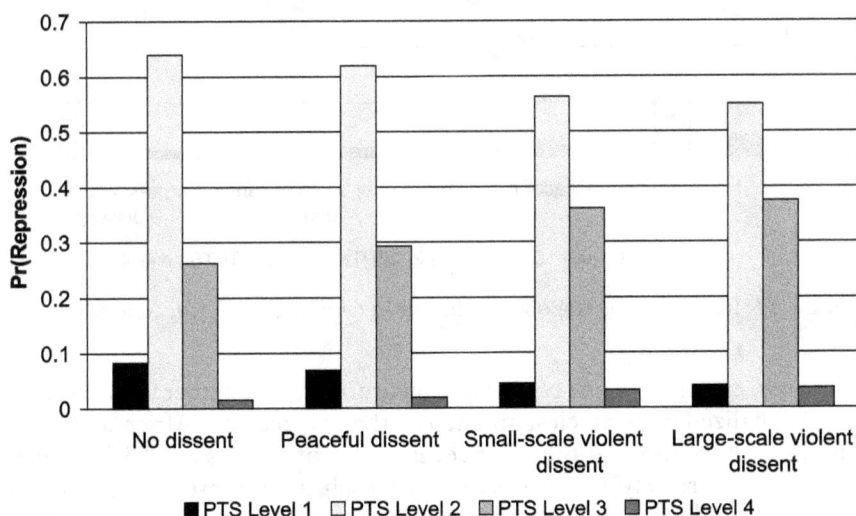

Figure 3.9 Repression as response to dissent in democracies, Africa.

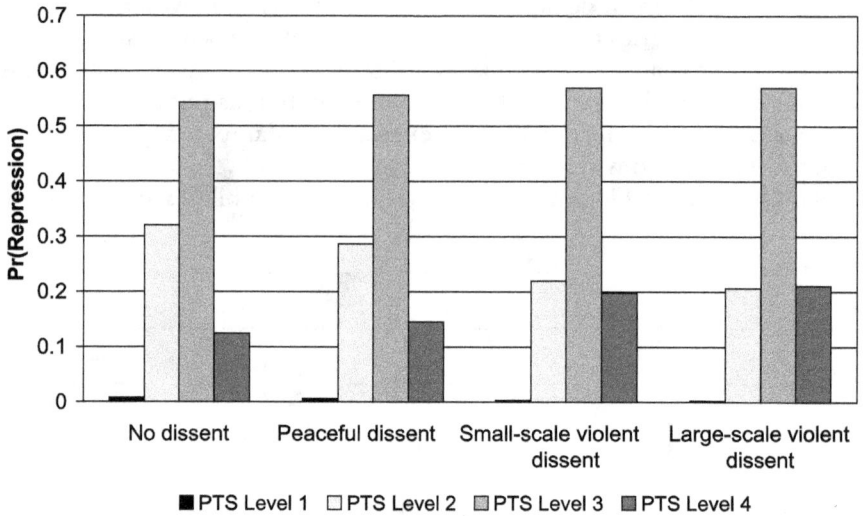

Figure 3.10 Repression as response to dissent in non-democracies, Latin America.

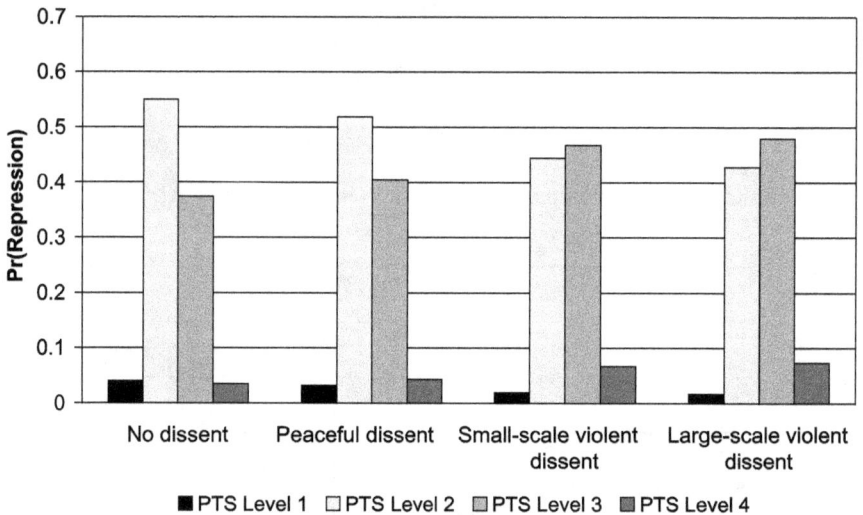

Figure 3.11 Repression as response to dissent in democracies, Latin America.

across two extreme regime types, fully institutionalized autocracies and fully institutionalized democracies, and across the two regions, Africa and Latin America. I have omitted the most severe form of repression (PTS Level 5) due to the extremely low probability of such a response. Note that the figures for authoritarian regimes use the label 'non-democracies'. I have chosen this term since the graphs for those regimes that are located in the middle of the autocracy–democracy spectrum are almost identical to those for full autocracies.

Graphing the relationship between dissent and repression for different regime types does not support the 'more murder in the middle' argument. These results show that regimes that are 'in the middle', combining both autocratic and democratic characteristics, are not more repressive than authoritarian regimes, irrespective of whether or not the regimes faces dissent. In semi-democracies, the response of government to dissent is the same as in fully authoritarian regimes.

These figures show that, compared to autocracies, democratic institutions have a pacifying effect on their governments in the domestic arena, supporting Hypothesis 3. In both regions, PTS Level 2 is more likely in democracies than in non-democracies. In Africa, even in the presence of violent dissent, the most likely reaction of a democratic government is rather limited coercion (PTS Level 2), while all other options are far less likely. In an authoritarian regime, however, the most likely response of the government to violent dissent is more widespread repression, as indicated by Level 3 of the Political Terror Scale. Hence, democracy in Africa is an effective instrument for 'softening' a government's response to domestic dissent.

This pacifying effect of democracy in the face of dissent takes on a slightly different form in Latin America, due to overall higher levels of repression. In non-democratic countries in Latin America, repression at PTS Level 3 is always by far the most likely outcome. In a democracy, the probability of PTS Level 3 is much lower. As in Africa, PTS Level 2 is the most likely level of repression in a democracy when no dissent or only peaceful dissent occurs, but when threatened with violent forms of dissent, the risk of more widespread repression at PTS Level 3 reaches almost 50 per cent. This is a higher probability than the predicted probability of PTS Level 2, but at a substantially smaller margin than in non-democracies. This tendency of Latin American governments to respond heavy-handedly to violent dissent is even more pronounced in authoritarian regimes. When faced with either small-scale or large-scale violent dissent, authoritarian governments in Latin America are almost equally likely to employ indiscriminate state terror (PTS Level 5) as limited repression (PTS Level 2), with the response at PTS Level 3 being by far the most likely outcome. For their African counterparts, even when faced with violent dissent, authoritarian governments are still far more likely to use limited repression (PTS Level 2) than indiscriminate state terror (PTS Level 5).

The impact of repression and political regimes on dissent

In this section, I turn the focus from explaining the level of repression to discussing the level of dissent. As with the model on state coercion, the analysis of dissent is based on a parsimonious model that includes the main independent variables that are theoretically important in this context and have received wide support in the quantitative literature in this field.[12] The results of this model, which was discussed in detail in the previous chapter, are presented in Table 3.6.[13]

As in the previous section, I first present the impact of the control variables before discussing how repression and regime type affect the probability of different levels of dissent. Table 3.6 shows that past dissent, political instability, civil war and population size are statistically significant and, as expected, increase the probability of dissent. The dummy variable for Africa is also statistically significant and indicates that the risk of dissent is lower in Africa than in Latin America. Table 3.7 shows the baseline model of dissent for an average Latin American and African country, as well as how the control variables change the predicted probabilities of dissent. The predicted probabilities of the two baseline models show again that the risk of dissent is lower in Africa compared to Latin America. The risk of large-scale violent dissent, when civil war and political instability are absent, is almost twice as high in Latin America as in Africa. While an African country has a 77.4 per cent chance of experiencing no dissent, and a 6.4 per cent risk of guerrilla warfare or rebellion, the comparable figures for a Latin American country are 67.4 per cent and 11.1 per cent respectively.

The overall impact of past dissent, political instability and civil war is

Table 3.6 Results of ordered probit model for dissent

	Coefficient	Robust std err.
Peaceful dissent$_{t-1}$	0.466***	0.094
Small-scale violent dissent$_{t-1}$	0.562***	0.093
Large-scale violent dissent$_{t-1}$	0.979***	0.094
PTS Level 2	0.224	0.135
PTS Level 3	0.559***	0.147
PTS Level 4	0.514**	0.166
PTS Level 5	0.961***	0.209
Democracy	0.030	0.029
Democracy^2	−0.001	0.001
Political instability	0.216*	0.086
Civil war	1.021***	0.113
Population size[a]	0.069*	0.030
Africa	−0.302***	0.075
τ_1	2.081	0.433
τ_2	2.452	0.435
τ_3	2.855	0.437
Log pseudolikelihood	−1497.098	
χ^2	580.66***	
Pseudo R^2	20.42	
N	1628	

a Variable log-transformed due to skewed distribution.
* $p < 0.05$, ** $p < 0.01$, *** $p < 0.001$, two-tailed tests.

Table 3.7 Changes in the predicted probabilities of dissent

	No dissent	Peaceful dissent	Small-scale violent dissent	Large-scale violent dissent	Average change
Latin America					
Baseline[a]	0.674	0.120	0.096	0.111	
Peaceful dissen$_{t-1}$	−0.183	0.005	0.030	0.148	0.092
Small-scale v. d.$_{t-1}$	−0.219	0.003	0.033	0.183	0.110
Large-scale v. d.$_{t-1}$	−0.372	0.006	0.054	0.312	0.186
Political instability	−0.086	0.005	0.016	0.065	0.043
Civil war	−0.359	−0.031	0.020	0.370	0.195
Africa					
Baseline[a]	0.774	0.095	0.067	0.064	
Peaceful dissen$_{t-1}$	−0.181	0.023	0.041	0.116	0.090
Small-scale v. d.$_{t-1}$	−0.219	0.025	0.048	0.145	0.109
Large-scale v. d.$_{t-1}$	−0.371	0.041	0.079	0.251	0.185
Political instability	−0.083	0.013	0.020	0.050	0.041
Civil war	−0.387	0.008	0.058	0.322	0.194

a The baseline does not represent changes in the predicted probabilities but the predicted probabilities of the baseline models. For this calculation, political instability and civil war were set at zero, all other variables at their mean.

Note: The figures in the last column 'Average change' represents the average of the absolute values of the changes across all four categories of the dissent scale.

almost identical across the two regions. In both regions, each form of past dissent increases the probability of protest. The more severe protest is in the current year, the larger is its impact on protest in the following year. It is interesting to note that large-scale violent rebellion is most substantially affected by previous levels of protest. For example, while in Africa peaceful anti-government demonstrations and strikes at time t-1 increase the risk of further peaceful dissent at time t by 0.023, those activities increase the probability of guerrilla warfare and rebellion by 0.116. In Latin America, when peaceful dissent occurs at time t-1, the probability of peaceful dissent at time t increases by 0.005, while the impact on the probability of large-scale violent dissent is almost 30 times higher, with an increase of 0.148. Less threatening protest activities often function as a precursor and build-up of more severe forms of dissent. In fact, when peaceful strikes or anti-government demonstrations occur, the most likely form of protest that follows is large-scale violent dissent. The most likely impact of peaceful protest is not that it continues, but that it escalates into large-scale violent dissent. This supports the argument that non-violent protest is often a precursor to violent protest. Violent forms of protest should not be seen in isolation. Tilly argues that 'violence ordinarily grows out of collective actions which are not intrinsically violent' (1978: 74). The same argument is also put forward by Gurr: 'Political action by minorities is a continuum; understanding its violent manifestations requires analysis of its nonviolent origins' (1993: 94). This notion is supported by the findings shown in Table 3.7.

Political instability has only a small impact on the probability of dissent. Civil war, however, has a particularly strong effect on the risk of large-scale violent dissent, but it also increases the risk of peaceful dissent and of riots. It is not surprising that during times of civil war, large-scale violent dissent in the form of rebellion and guerrilla warfare becomes far more likely. Rebellions are often treated as synonymous with civil wars, although they are different, albeit related, concepts. Both civil war and large-scale violent dissent refer to periods of violence that involve non-state actors. But whereas rebellion is a one-sided, or unilateral, concept, as it focuses only on the behaviour of the non-state, civil war is an inherently dynamic and bi- or multi-lateral concept in that it involves at least two actors, one representing the government and one representing non-governmental forces.[14]

The impact of political instability, civil war and past dissent is very similar across both regions. The main difference is how these factors impact upon peaceful dissent. While any type of past dissent and political instability increases the probability of peaceful dissent only marginally in Latin America, this positive impact is far more substantial in Africa. For example, while large-scale violent dissent at time t-1 increases peaceful dissent by 0.006 in Latin America, the effect in Africa is almost seven times larger, with an increase of 0.41. The difference is most pronounced with respect to civil war. During a civil war in Latin America, peaceful protest becomes less likely, while it increases by 0.013 in Africa. In Latin America, it appears to be rather difficult to motivate people to participate in strikes and demonstrations with past protests or during a civil war; instead, they are more likely to participate in more extreme forms of dissent. But in the end we are roughly equally likely to see demonstrations and strikes on both continents since the baseline probability of peaceful dissent is higher in Latin America than in Africa.

But how do people respond when they are faced with government coercion? In Table 3.6 we can see that all levels of repression, apart from PTS Level 2, are statistically significant at $p < 0.01$ or better. This mirrors the findings of the repression model, where the least intense and least threatening form of dissent – peaceful strikes and demonstrations – did not have a statistically significant effect on repression. In the model of dissent, the lowest and most restrained form of state coercion, PTS Level 2, which stands for limited political imprisonment and only rare instances of torture and killings, also fails to reach conventional levels of statistical significance. But the more severe levels of repression, PTS Levels 3 to 5, are highly statistically significant and positive, indicating that repression increases dissent.

Figure 3.12 shows the changes in the predicted probabilities of dissent when the government employs different levels of coercion in comparison to the absence of any repression (which is why the category PTS Level 1 is not represented in the graph). Since the changes in the predicted probabilities are

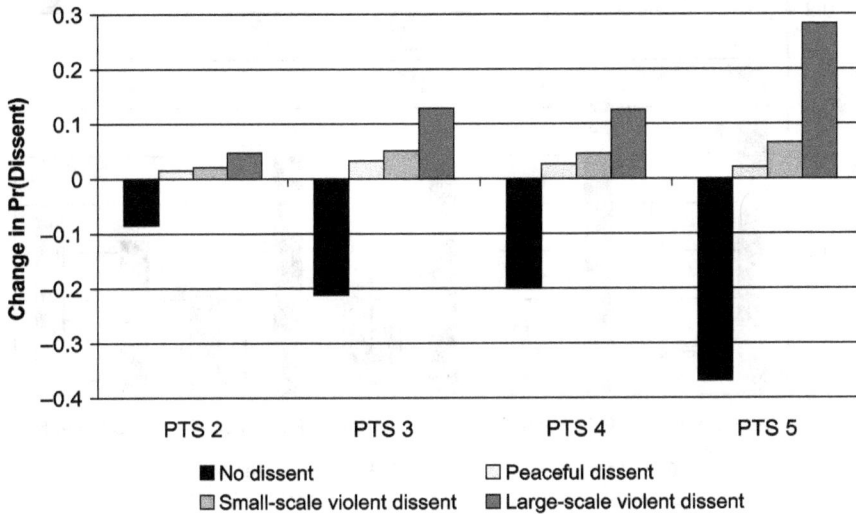

Figure 3.12 Change in predicted probabilities of dissent in Africa.

almost identical for Africa and Latin America, I show only the graph for Africa. The main difference between the two regions is that the predicted probability of peaceful dissent decreases under PTS Level 5 in Latin America, while it increases in Africa. But the absolute values of the changes are very small.[15] The main message from Figure 3.12 is that under any form of life integrity violations, whether widespread and indiscriminate, or whether taking place only as isolated and targeted events, the chances that no dissent occurs, decline. At the same time, the probability of some form of dissent increases, and it increases by a larger margin the more severe repression is. The more severe repression is, the more likely more severe forms of dissent become. This supports Hypothesis 5, which argued that repression increases the probability of dissent. These figures suggest that any form of repression spurs on organized and violent rebellion. This result is in contrast with the argument that under very repressive regimes, the costs and risks associated with dissent prevent people from initiating and participating in protest against the government (Muller and Weede 1990).

Merely looking at the changes in the predicted probabilities does not tell us which types of dissent are actually most likely to occur under the different levels of repression. Figures 3.13 and 3.14 plot the predicted probabilities of no dissent and the three different forms of dissent under varying levels of repression for Latin America and Africa. The graphs show again that as repression becomes more severe, the chances of no dissent decrease and the risk of more violent dissent increases. But in almost all scenarios, no dissent is still the most likely outcome, by a rather substantial margin. This might seem like a gamble that repressive governments are willing to take: although

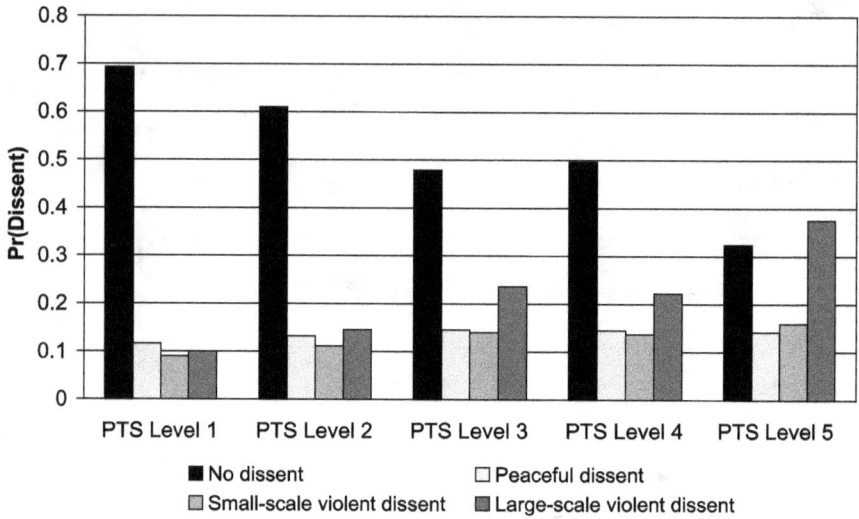

Figure 3.13 Dissent as response to repression in Latin America.

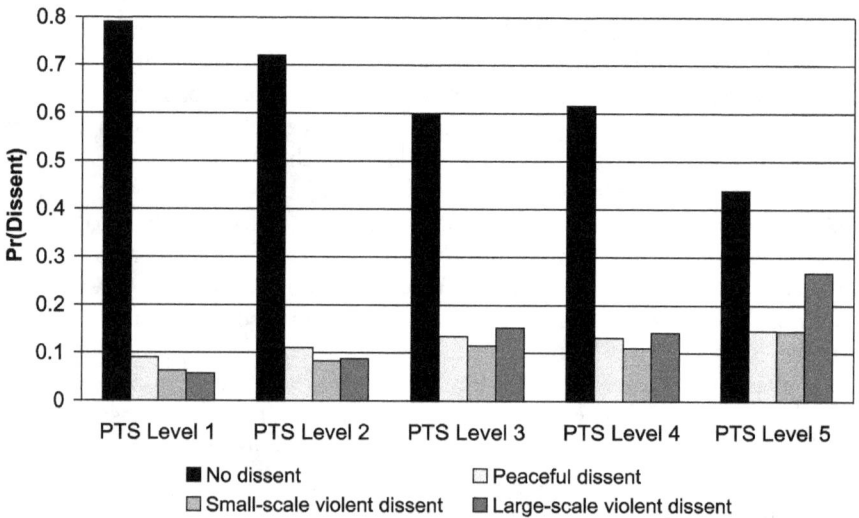

Figure 3.14 Dissent as response to repression in Africa.

the use of repression increases the risk that the population 'retaliates' with dissent, the most likely outcome is still that the population stays at home and does not participate in dissent and protest activities.

There is one exception to this scenario. In Latin America, when governments kill their citizens on a large scale the most likely response is large-scale violent dissent. Figure 3.13 shows that at PTS Level 5, large-scale violent protest has the highest predicted probabilities, although by a small margin. The probability of no dissent in Latin American countries with repression at PTS Level 5 is 0.325, while the probability of large-scale violent dissent is 0.375. But, in general, opposition is difficult to mobilize into physical acts against the government. The problem of collective action is hard to overcome, even when the government violates the basic right of its citizens. Figures 3.13 and 3.14 confirm, however, what had already become evident from the changes in the predicted probabilities shown in Figure 3.12. Repression does not function as a deterrent to dissent. Protest activities do not become *less* likely during times of repression, but instead are more likely to be carried out against the government. Hence, governments would be ill advised to assume that they could minimize potential domestic threats in the form of dissent by torturing and killing their opponents.

In the previous chapter I argued that more democratic regimes should be less likely to experience dissent because regime opponents have certain institutions and mechanisms available to them to voice their discontent (H_6). At the same time, the expectation that opposition demands are heard and accommodated, rather than being overlooked and ignored, is higher in democracies than in non-democracies. Table 3.6 does not, however, support this argument, as the variables for institutional democracy are not statistically significant. Although the signs of the coefficients hint at an inverted U-shaped relationship between degree of democracy and dissent, the standard errors are too large to draw any meaningful conclusions from these results. Instead, the results suggest that the level of democracy makes no noticeable difference to the protest behaviour of people in Latin America or Africa. One possible explanation might be that while in democracies opposition forces have institutionalized channels for voicing discontent available to them, the anticipated risk of being severely punished for protest activities is low in such democratic regimes. Hence, the higher 'need' for dissent might be counterbalanced by a higher risk attached to these activities in non-democratic regimes.

Hypothesis 7 argued that, in democracies, the opposition should be more likely to protest against the use of repression than in non-democracies. But the use of dissent in response to repression seems to be independent of regime type. The changes in the predicted probabilities of dissent as response to repression, calculated for an autocratic regime, a semi-democracy and a democracy, are very similar. Figures A.1 to A.3 in the Appendix show the predicted probabilities of dissent in Latin America for an authoritarian regime (Figure A.1), a semi-democracy (Figure A.2) and a democracy (Figure A.3). When repression occurs, the probability of no dissent is lower in more democratic countries, but the difference is rather small and becomes negligible once confidence intervals are taken into account.[16] The figures also suggest that when a government in an autocratic regime uses widespread repression at PTS Level 5, people are most likely to stay at home, whereas in a semi-democracy and in a democracy, large-scale violent dissent becomes the most likely response under such circumstances. However, given the small difference in the respective predicted probabilities and the relatively large confidence intervals, these results are rather tenuous. Therefore, Hypothesis 7, which expected that, in democracies, the opposition is more likely to respond to repression with protest than in non-democracies, finds only very weak support in the empirical analysis.

SUMMARY

This chapter has presented and discussed the results of a large-N analysis of Latin America and Africa from 1977 to 2002, which investigated how dissent affects repression and how repression influences dissent. The analysis lent support to most arguments put forward in the previous chapter. Dissent increases the risk of repression and repression increases the risk of dissent. The results also suggest that a more serious threat triggers a more severe response. Violent dissent, whether spontaneous, as in the form of riots, or whether more organized and large-scale, as in the form of guerrilla warfare, substantially increases the risk of repression. The impact of peaceful dissent on state coercion appears to be negligible. Violent protest against a government is a dangerous strategy and is generally met with force. As predicted by the theory, governments try to minimize threats in form of dissent by increasing the level of repression that they use against citizens and their opponents. Similarly, when governments employ widespread repression, the opposition is likely to respond with force as well. The more violent and widespread the repression used by the government, the more likely violent and large-scale forms of dissent become. This suggests that the actions by one actor are met with very similar reactions by the other. The relationship between protest and repression is not, however, strictly linear, based on the categories used in this analysis. Governments respond to any kind of violent dissent in the same way. Whether violent protest occurs on a smaller scale and is spontaneous, as in the form of riots, or whether violent protest is carried out on a larger scale in the form of guerrilla warfare or rebellion, governments use similar levels of repression to respond to these violent types of dissent. The most threatening feature of dissent, therefore, appears to be whether dissent is violent or not. With respect to dissent as a reaction to repression, the risk of dissent appears to be almost identical for PTS Levels 3 and 4. For both levels of state coercion, the possibility of no dissent decreases and the risk of some dissent increases to very similar degrees. Once repression has crossed a certain threshold, but where state terror has not yet been extended to the whole population, the impact on dissent behaviour is the same.

The results have also shown that while democracy is an effective way of reducing the risk of state coercion, it has no impact upon dissident behaviour. The most democratic countries have a substantially lower risk of widespread repression than less democratic countries, but no clear impact could be detected on the risk of protest activities. The results suggest that this pacifying effect of democracy on their governments kicks in only when democratic features are solidly embedded in the regime. Countries that find themselves closer to the middle of the autocracy–democracy spectrum fare not much better than the most autocratic countries. This finding supports the threshold argument put forward by Davenport and Armstrong (2004), which posits that only the most democratic countries benefit from the pacifying effect of democratic institutions. Democracy also seems to be effective in taming governments' responses to threat. Autocracies and semi-democracies react much more harshly to dissent than do democracies. Although in democracies the risk of repression still increases when the government finds itself confronted with violent dissent, this increase is lower compared to countries that do not benefit from thoroughly entrenched democratic institutions.

The results have shown that the relationship between protest and repression is relatively similar in both Latin America and sub-Saharan Africa during the observed time period. The main difference is that Latin American governments were more repressive than their African counterparts. This is mainly influenced by widespread government violence during the 1980s in Latin America, which is reflected in Figure 3.1. This more violent behaviour of Latin American compared to African leaders remains consistent even if one takes into account the type of dissent that governments are faced with, or the degree of democracy under which they operate. Non-democratic Latin American countries are more repressive than African non-democracies, and Latin American democracies are more repressive than African democracies. The pacifying effect of democracy on government behaviour kicks in earlier, i.e. for less democratic regimes, in Africa than in Latin America. When faced with violent dissent, Latin American governments are also more likely to react more harshly than are African governments. The most likely behaviour of Latin American governments is the use of repression at PTS Level 3 (which refers to extensive political imprisonment and political killings being relatively common), and the gap to the next likely outcome, which is a less violent government response at PTS Level 2, increases under more severe forms of dissent. In Africa, however, the probability of PTS Levels 2 and 3 is almost the same when no dissent occurs or when dissent remains peaceful. Only when faced with violent forms of protest, does repression at PTS Level 3 become the most likely outcome. But the gap to PTS Level 2 is far smaller in Africa than in Latin America. The chance that state coercion is carried out at a very limited level is higher in Africa than in Latin America, even when governments find themselves threatened by domestic dissent.

While governments are more repressive in Latin America than in Africa, the opposition is also more active in staging protests in Latin America compared to Africa. In over 60 per cent of the African sample no dissent occurs, while in Latin America dissent is absent in less than 40 per cent of the sample. However, when it comes to guerrilla warfare and rebellion, both regions have very similar records during the observed time period. When governments

employ widespread repression, the opposition in Latin America is more likely
to respond with large-scale violent dissent compared to Africa.

Notes

1 Examples of other studies that have focused on particular regions are Aflatooni
   and Allen (1991), Francisco (1995), Gartner and Regan (1996), Schatzman
   (2005) and Swaminathan (1999).
2 As discussed in the previous chapter, a dummy variable for African countries
   is included in the analyses to account for systematic differences between the two
   regions under investigation.
3 For a list of publications that have used this measure, see http://
   www.politicalterrorscale.org/bibliography.html.
4 See http://www.databanksinternational.com/.
5 The coding of the original count variables from Banks' archive is based on only one
   new source, the *New York Times*, and is therefore bound to miss certain events,
   making a binary measure arguably more reliable than an account measure.
6 Schatzman (2005) employs a similar strategy in grouping together Banks' variables on domestic conflict, but she creates two measures – collective protest
   and rebellion – where collective protest is made up of demonstrations, strikes and
   riots, and rebellion of assassinations, guerrilla warfare and rebellion.
7 As mentioned in the previous chapter, the correlation between civil war and
   dissent is 0.548 and the variance inflation factor is 1.43.
8 The alternative method is ordered logit. The main difference between the two
   models is the distribution of the error term. In practice, the results obtain from an
   ordered probit or logit model are usually substantively the same (Long 1997). For
   a detailed discussion of ordered probit, see Long (1997) in particular, but also
   Greene (2000).
9 To test a potential time delay in the impact of dissent on repression, I used
   dissent at t-1 in a separate analysis, but the lagged dissent indicators were not
   statistically significant. In a separate analysis, I also included a dummy variable
   for international war, which has widely been used in the quantitative human
   rights literature. But this variable does not reach statistical significance, which
   could be due to the rare occurrence of civil war in the sample.
10 For these calculations, all variables were set at their mean or, in the case of binary
   variables, at their model value zero.
11 To calculate these predicted probabilities, all values are set at their mean, apart
   from political instability and civil war being held constant at zero.
12 Additional control variables that have widely been used in the literature on rebellion and civil war include ethnic heterogeneity, population density and moun-
   tainous terrain, generally producing mixed results (e.g. Buhaug 2006; Carey
   2007; Fearon and Laitin 2003; Hegre and Sambanis 2006; Hegre *et al.* 2001). In
   a robustness test, I include measures for these three factors, but neither comes
   close to commonly used levels of statistical significance.
13 Before discussing the results of the statistical analysis of dissent, some brief
   remarks about endogeneity are in order. One of the main arguments of this
   research is that dissent leads to repression and that repression leads to dissent.
   Based on this hypothesis, I employ vector autoregression for the statistical analysis presented in Chapter 4. Here, I use ordered probit techniques to estimate the
   models of dissent and repression. To account for the endogeneity in the models,
   simultaneous equations are the standard textbook suggestions for statistical
   analysis. However, the main problem with this approach is that results are heavily
   dependent upon the choice of the model and, more specifically, on the choice of

the instrumental variables. Due to the nature of the main three variables in this research design, it is rather difficult to think of an appropriate set of instrumental variables that are closely related to the main independent variables but independent of the dependent variables. Therefore, I did not use simultaneous equation models for the analysis. However, I used three-stage least squares regressions to compare the results with those obtained from the ordered probit analysis, and there were no substantive differences. Additionally, simultaneous equation models, such as three-stage least squares regression, do not account for the potential non-linearity of ordinal variables, as used in this analysis. But the ability of ordered probit models to accommodate non-linear relationships is theoretically particularly interesting in the context of this research.

14 For a similar distinction between unilateral and bilateral types of violence, see Kalyvas (2006: 29).

15 $\Pr_{\text{Latin America}}(\text{Peaceful Dissent}|\text{PTS=5}) = -0.016$ and $\Pr_{\text{Africa}}(\text{Peaceful Dissent}|\text{PTS=5}) = 0.021$.

16 The 95 per cent confidence intervals are not included in the figures.

4 A dynamic model of protest and repression[1]

The previous chapter investigated how protest affects repression and how repression affects protest. Both relationships have been treated and analysed separately from each other, an approach that is reflected in the majority of research on protest and repression. This chapter provides an analysis that is specifically tailored to analysing the interaction between protest and repression. It follows an approach used by Davis and Ward (1990), who employ an inductive method to analyse the dynamics of domestic violent conflict. Using quarterly data, they study the protest–repression nexus in Chile. In the following, I develop a model of domestic conflict and accommodation that pays particular attention to the dynamic interaction between government and non-government actors. Subsequently, I introduce the data, which are taken from the Intranational Political Interactions (IPI) project by Davis, Leeds and Moore (Davis et al. 1998). The data capture daily events in six countries from Latin America (Argentina, Brazil, Chile, Colombia, Mexico and Venezuela) and in three countries from sub-Saharan Africa (Nigeria, Zaire and Zimbabwe) over an approximately 12-year period between the late 1970s and the early 1990s. Chapter 5 then discusses the methodology and presents the empirical results of vector autoregression (VAR) models.

The main advantage of this analysis is the explicit focus on the dynamic interaction between dissent and repression. As the analysis in the previous chapter has already shown, both dissent and state coercion influence each other. If we want to find out why people protest against their governments, we ought to take into account how governments react towards them. Similarly, if we want to better understand why states torture and kill their citizens, we ought to investigate the behaviour of the population towards their governments. The theoretical model and the empirical investigation presented in this chapter put particular emphasis on these dynamics.

The second advantage of the analysis presented in this chapter is that cooperative behaviour is added into the equation of protest and repression. Lichbach (1987: 294) concludes that in order to adequately analyse the protest–repression nexus, accommodating strategies should be included in the model. The previous chapter, like most previous research in this field, has focused on different levels of conflictual behaviour without accounting for cooperative actions. In this chapter, I investigate how accommodating behaviour of one actor influences the hostile behaviour of the other actor. The third advantage is the use of more temporally disaggregated data. The analysis presented in the previous chapter used yearly data to investigate the relationship between protest and repression (see also Davenport 1995; Gupta *et al.* 1993). However, the interaction between the government and the opposition is often much more immediate. To reflect the dynamic interaction between the government and opposition forces, I use daily data for the following analysis. Due to moving to daily observations, the analysis in this chapter does not include any control variables, since they barely change on a daily level. Another main difference is that after the macro-level investigation of how dissent impacts upon repression and how repression influences dissent, the following analysis disaggregates the actors' behaviour into cooperative and conflictual actions, and studies the dynamics in nine individual countries separately without aggregating over the countries.

DYNAMIC MODEL OF INTERNAL CONFLICT

Two main conclusions can be drawn from the theories in the field of domestic conflict that were presented in Chapter 2. First, the theories generally concentrate on only one direction of the relationship between protest and repression, and ignore the effect that the dependent variable might have on the independent variable. For example, deterrence theory argues that higher repression leads to lower levels of protest because protest becomes too costly. In repressive regimes, people are too afraid to show dissent and voice opposition, out of fear of the repercussions. This theoretical approach does not take account of the possibility that the behaviour of the government might also be influenced by the behaviour of the dissidents. Similarly, the backlash hypothesis argues that very low and very high levels of state coercion lead to high levels of protest, whereas protest is lowest under 'medium' levels of repression. Again, the backlash excludes the impact that protest has on repression from the analysis of the conflictual behaviour of the population.

The second main conclusion that can be drawn from the discussion of theories on protest and repression is that even when focusing on only one direction of the relationship, there is no superior theory on how the relationship should look. Rather, there is a variety of contradicting theoretical arguments that account for almost all possible relationships between protest and repression – and most of them are supported by empirical findings. There is no theory that would identify the direction in which the arrow of causality should go, if the relationship between protest and repression was only unidirectional. Additionally, the results of the ordered probit analysis presented in the previous chapter suggested that an increase in protest increases the probability of violent state response, and that an increase in repression increases the probability of widespread protest. The time-series analysis in this chapter builds upon the two main conclusions from the theories on repression and dissent, and on the findings presented above.

The two main arguments that the analysis in this chapter builds upon are that the relationship between protest and repression is dynamic and interactive, and that there are no clear theoretical arguments in the prior literature on how this relationship should look. This means that I expect the causal arrow between protest and repression to go both ways. If we want to find out why people engage in protest against their government, we ought to take into account the government's behaviour towards its people, how it deals with opposition and dissent. Similarly, if we want to look at why governments restrict the freedom of their citizens, or even torture and kill them, it is important to include the behaviour of the opposition towards the government in the analysis. In short, in order to explain the impact of state coercion on protest, we ought to take into account the effect protest has on state coercion; and in order to analyse the impact of protest on state repression, we ought to take into account the effect repression has on protest.

The first criterion for choosing the appropriate statistical methodology for this study is that it has to accommodate the two-way relationship between protest and repression. Since specific hypotheses on the relationship between protest and repression have not yielded a consistent picture, I focus on two questions: whether protest affects repression and whether repression affects protest. Therefore, the second criterion of the method used to analyse the dynamics of domestic conflict has to be flexible so that it does not impose a certain type of relationship that is based on weak theoretical grounding.

The core argument put forward in this section is that protest and repression cannot be seen in isolation, but are connected by a dynamic interdependence. Protest and repression are interdependent. The behaviour of the opposition towards the government is influenced by the way in which the government reacts to the behaviour of the opposition. Similarly, the behaviour of the government towards dissent is conditioned on the action of the opposition towards the government. Both actors are expected to imitate each other's behaviour, similar to a tit-for-tat strategy (e.g. Axelrod 1985; Leng 1984). As results in the previous chapter have shown, if the population is faced with repression, citizens become more likely to show dissent. Similarly, if the government encounters protest, it is expected to respond with repression.

The government and the opposition orientate their actions primarily on the observable behaviour of the opponent, because the situation under which both actors operate is marked by limited information, limited capabilities and uncertain payoffs. Although both actors might be aware of each other's agenda, they will most likely have only limited information about their persistence and the resources that are available to them to pursue their goals. For example, dissidents often do not know whether hardliners or softliners are more powerful within the government. There is typically a significant amount of uncertainty about how much protest can be mobilized by the opposition forces. Hence, the payoffs of certain strategies are usually uncertain. With this background, both actors use each other's behaviour to guide their own actions.

When faced with government sanctions or coercion, dissidents are expected to respond with resistance. Analysing the Iranian Revolution, Rasler (1996) argues that due to micromobilization processes, protest increases in the long run when faced with government sanctions. Micro-mobilization occurs because overt dissident behaviour shows the willingness and commitment of others, it makes the goal of their activities desirable, and raises the social rewards for participating in the dissent movement (Chong 1991; Opp 1994). Opp and Roehl argue that 'repression sets in motion "micromobilization processes" that raise the rewards and diminish the costs of participation' (1990: 523). The reaction of the government to dissident activities is expected to be similar to the response of dissidents to repression. If a government is faced with protest, it is likely to respond with coercion in order to reduce the threat posed by such dissent.

The second argument is that accommodation influences hostile actions. With some exceptions, accommodating behaviour has largely been ignored in studies on the protest–repression nexus. Lichbach (1987) models the use of different government strategies and concludes that consistent policies, i.e. employing either coercion or accommodation consistently, decrease dissent, whereas inconsistent policies, i.e. using both coercive and accommodating tactics, increase it because they send mixed messages to the opposition. Rasler (1996) finds support for the argument that government concessions increase protest. This hypothesis is based on the value-expectancy model, which states that if people expect protest to achieve the desired public good, they are more likely to participate in dissent activities (e.g. Muller and Opp 1986). If governments make concessions to the opposition, it raises the expectation that the opposition's goal will be achieved, which in turn encourages people to participate in dissent activities. Following this argu-ment, I expect that accommodating state behaviour increases dissent. Being confronted by a cooperative government lowers the costs of protest and potentially raises the benefits. Government accommodation can also be interpreted as a weakness of the state that is to be taken advantage of in the form of dissent.

When dissidents show accommodating behaviour, governments, on the other hand, are expected not to respond with repression since this might backfire and turn further sections of the population against the regime, as argued in the backlash hypothesis. The backlash hypothesis argues that extremely severe coercion, although it decreases protest temporarily, increases dissident behaviour in the long run, especially when repression is applied indiscriminately (Mason and Krane 1989). Repression also carries international costs – for example, in the form of international shaming or sanctions. International costs are likely to be particularly high when governments repress an opposition that shows signs of cooperating with the regime. Hence, I expect that accommodation by dissidents does not lead to repression.

As argued in Chapter 2, and supported by the findings of the general analysis in Chapter 3, both protest and repression are expected to continue once they have been started. Policy inertia dampens radical changes in the government's behaviour. The government tends to maintain strategies once they have been adopted. Government agencies also try to perpetuate their existence. When special security forces are put in place to protect the national executive and to control dissident groups, they usually try to maintain their status and are difficult to dissolve. Protest movements tend to maintain themselves as well. The threshold model suggests that once the number of participants crosses a particular threshold, the costs of mobilizing a larger crowd decline. Once dissidents have successfully invested in organizing and carrying out dissent, the costs of maintaining momentum and sustaining protest decline. Similarly, the bandwagon model suggests that once a critical mass of protesters is achieved, more people are likely to join because they feel encouraged by the protesters' commitment and willingness to dissent (e.g. Muller and Opp 1986; Rasler 1996).

Various arguments, including the bandwagon model, the threshold model and micromobilization processes, suggest that both protest and repression constantly increase. So why do we generally not expect to see them spiralling out of control? Escalation of repression is hindered by the costs and dangers of widespread and large-scale repression. Severe coercion carries domestic and international costs. It requires a well-equipped, loyal and large repressive apparatus, which is difficult and expensive to maintain. Indiscriminate and continuous repression is likely to trigger a backlash and to increase resistance from the opposition (Francisco 1995). International costs include being subject to blaming and shaming by other countries and international organizations, as well as isolation and exclusion from international bodies and the termination of trade relations.[2]

There are also barriers to stop dissent from endlessly escalating. The most obvious is the limited pool of potential protesters. Of course the realistic pool of potential dissidents is generally lower than the size of the population. And although people are more likely to join an already ongoing protest, if the group of dissidents grows extremely large, problems of coordination and communication start to kick in. Therefore, although both protest and repression are expected to maintain themselves in the short run, they are not expected to escalate or continue indefinitely.

REGIME TYPE AS CONDITIONING FACTOR

As outlined earlier, the dynamics of domestic conflict and cooperation are likely to differ under different institutional settings. Political regimes set the rules of the game and shape the interaction between government and opposition. They determine the choice of actors and the costs attached to this choice. Authoritarian regimes usually do not have institutionalized channels that accommodate popular discontent and opposition. The norms and institutions that are in place in democracies are designed to facilitate compromise and accommodation. This tends to keep the level of conflict comparatively low. For the following analysis, I divide countries into three categories: democracies, semi-democracies and non-democracies (also called 'autocracies' and 'authoritarian regimes' in the following). These labels refer to the degree of political participation and competition (Dahl 1971).

As argued earlier, and supported by the results presented in the previous chapter, I expect that, in democracies, repression is less likely to follow protest than in other regimes. Democracies are not only institutionally restrained from using repression or negative sanctions, but democratic norms also favour dialogue when faced with opposition. Democracies are also less likely to perceive domestic dissent as a threat (Davenport 1999). As such, they are expected to be less likely to reciprocate popular protest with repression (e.g. Rummel 1997). Although the general analysis in the previous chapter did not provide support for the argument that regime type impacts upon dissident behaviour, further disaggregating data might be able to uncover a link between degree of democracy and dissent. I expect that in democratic regimes, people are more likely to reciprocate repression with dissent than in other regimes. In countries with democratic institutions, citizens enjoy a certain set of rights and protection from the government. When a government steps over the line, the population is likely to protest against the infringement of their rights and liberties. Additionally, due to democratic norms of non-violent conflict resolution, the costs of dissent are expected to be lower in democracies than in non-democracies. I expect that in authoritarian regimes repression is less likely to systematically lead to protest. Autocratic regimes are inherently less prone to accommodate the demands of their citizens since their institutions and procedures are set up to avoid popular accountability and responsiveness. Therefore, the benefits of dissent are likely to be low, while the costs of protest as a response to repression are expected to be very high. Finally, accommodating state behaviour is expected to be most consistent in democracies compared to other regimes. Because of the democratic norms and institutions mentioned above, accommodation of the opposition should be a more constant feature of government actions than in non-democracies.

To sum up, I expect that the opposition responds with protest to repression and the government responds with repression to protest, and that both types of conflictual behaviour continue. Taking into account the differences between regime types, democracies are expected to be less likely than other regimes to see repression as a response to protest, but more likely to experience protest as a response to repression. Autocracies are argued to be less likely to experience protest when employing repression. Additionally, accommodating state behaviour is expected to be autoregressive in democracies. Overall, dissidents are hypothesized to respond to state accommodation with protest, whereas governments are expected not to display conflictual actions when faced with dissident accommodation.

INTRODUCING THE DATA

In the analysis in the previous chapter, domestic conflict was understood as open physical acts of confrontation. Attention was focused on physical behaviour and interactions between the government and the opposition. This definition is extended in the following analysis to also include non-physical actions, such as verbal threats and statements. With respect to dissent, Tilly argues that 'group violence ordinarily grows out of collective actions which are not intrinsically violent – festivals, meetings, strikes, demonstrations and so on. Without them, the collective violence could hardly occur' (1978: 74). Similarly, on the side of the government, the concept of coercion is extended to include non-physical actions, such as deadlock in negations, since 'all address behaviour that is applied by governments in an effort to bring about political quiescence and facilitate the continuity of the regime through some form of restriction or violation of political and civil liberties' (Davenport 2000: 6). The advantage of restricting the observation of behaviour to physical acts only, which was done in the previous chapters, is that such physical acts are usually based on a stronger commitment and intent than verbal statements, for example. People are probably more likely to say something they do not fully mean or they would not follow up with actions, whereas undertaking confrontational actions is likely to be a better indicator of the actual intentions of the actors.[3] But including these 'less intense' forms of behaviour allows us to investigate how the government and the opposition respond to each other's non-physical behaviours in order to find out whether such interactions follow a similar pattern as the dynamics of physical acts of confrontation and conflict.

To analyse the dynamic relationship between domestic protest and state repression, I use data from the Intranational Political Interactions (IPI) Project (Davis *et al.* 1998; Moore 1998, 2000). This project measures intrastate political conflict and cooperation on a ten-point scale by coding a range of different news sources (Reuters North American Service, Reuters World Service, the *New York Times* Index and the Africa Research Bulletin). It identifies the actor, target and intensity of the events, which are listed by day of occurrence. One can therefore identify who is doing what to whom on a daily basis. The data cover nine middle powers from Latin America and Africa between 1974 and 1992. They include a broad spectrum of state actors, such as the executive, the military, paramilitary forces and the police. They also identify a variety of non-state actors, such as specific ethnic populations, dissident organizations, labour unions and churches. The data capture a wide breadth of conflictual behaviour, ranging from non-violent, low-confrontational actions to large-scale killings and civil war.[4]

I have chosen the IPI dataset for three main reasons. First, it corresponds extremely well with the research questions that I am interested in. The variables of the IPI dataset closely capture the interaction between government and non-government actors, and clearly identify who does what to whom and when. Second, this dataset covers an interesting set of countries, as discussed in further detail in the Appendix. Nine countries from Latin America and Africa are coded for a time period of eight to thirteen years. The variables on protest and repression vary substantially within and between the countries. The nine countries also cover the whole spectrum of authoritarian regimes; for example, they include various forms of authoritarianism under Pinochet in Chile and military regimes in Nigeria, as well as various democratic regimes, such as re-established democracies in Argentina and Brazil in the 1980s, and Zimbabwe after independence. Moreover, some of them have experienced more regime changes than others during the time period of observation. Together they represent an interesting sample of countries with different backgrounds and experiences with domestic political conflict and democracy. The socio-political backgrounds of the nine countries are explored in more detail in the Appendix. Concentrating on nine countries allows me to conduct separate analyses of each of them and then to compare the results. In contrast to the macro-level analysis in the previous chapter, I do not pool the data, in order to pay closer attention to the events and interactions within each state.

The issue of temporal aggregation is the third main reason for choosing the IPI dataset. The IPI data allow me to build a daily dataset. Choosing the level of aggregation that most closely reflects the data-generating process substantially contributes to the validity of the empirical results produced by statistical analysis (Freeman 1989). Other studies have employed weekly data to imitate the data-generating process more closely (e.g. Francisco 1995, 1996; Rasler 1996), while some researchers use the concept of turns and moves to avoid the problem of temporal aggregation, but end up ignoring the temporal aspect of interaction (e.g. Moore 1998, 2000).

The interaction between the government and the population, the dynamics between protest and repression, take place within a specific setting. As Davenport (2000) argues, both repression and protest are influenced by contextual factors, such as by the general political and socio-economic characteristics of the environment. Due to the lack of appropriate data, I cannot account for these variations and effects in the statistical analysis. But since these elements function as implicit control variables, I discuss them in more detail in the Appendix. In the following, I give a short summary of the main characteristics of the nine countries.

With the exception of Argentina, which has a relatively homogeneous society, all other countries are more ethnically fractionalized, with Zaire and Nigeria's populations being the most heterogeneous. Also, the level of urbanization is very similar across all cases, with the exception of Nigeria. On average, almost 95 per cent of the population lived in urban areas during the time period of the study. Looking at the economic background of the nine countries, one main pattern emerges: the division based on average GNP per capita during the time period of the study along regional lines, which was also reflected in the macro-level analysis. The three African countries are substantially poorer than the Latin American ones. Looking more closely at the economic performances of the nine countries, a more diverse picture emerges. Argentina, Brazil and Chile were faced with extremely high inflation rates and increasing unemployment during the period of observation. Their inflation rates were not matched by those of the other Latin American countries, Colombia, Mexico and Venezuela, which also encountered economic crises in the 1980s. The main problems the African economies had to tackle were debt crises and corruption. Although the Latin American countries had a far higher GNP per capita than the African ones, they had their share of serious economic crises as well. The nine countries encountered different levels of domestic political conflict, as well as different experiences with varying degrees of democracy.

The IPI Scale codes news sources ranging from −1 to −10 for conflictual and 1 to 10 for accommodating behaviour.[5] The conflict scale includes mildly negative statements (−1), riots (−4), as well as civil war (−10). The accommodation scale ranges from statements of support (1), to agreements to talk (4), to conflict resolution (10). For the analysis, I transform these ordinal-level data into interval-like data, based on Shellman (2004). Shellman asked experts to rank a list of events taken from the original IPI scale from least to most cooperative and from least to most hostile, and then to assign each event a weight from 1 to 100. The final scales consist of the average weights assigned by the experts. Table 4.1 shows the original value, the weight and the description of the ranked conflictual events, and Table 4.2 gives these details for cooperative events.[6]

I create four new variables for each of the nine countries, two variables for hostile events and two for accommodating actions, depending on who the actor and who the target is. The variable measuring hostile actions of the government towards the population is labelled 'repression'; the one measuring hostile actions of the population towards the government is labelled 'protest'. These two variables are multiplied by minus one to arrive at positive values, with higher values indicating more severe conflict. The third variable is labelled 'dissident accommodation' and captures accommodation of the government by the opposition, while 'state accommodation' measures accommodating actions by the government. The activities are measured on a daily basis.[7] If more than one event is recorded for one of the four variables, I use only the most severe, i.e. the most accommodating or the most hostile event.[8] Violent and non-violent conflictual actions are seen as part of one continuum, rather than two separate forms of dissent,

Table 4.1 Details of conflict variables

Original value	Weight	Description
−1	−4.12	Group X criticizes Government Y's new policy
−2	−7.88	Government X rejects opposition Group Y's proposals for reform
−3	−12.71	Group X demonstrates non-violently against Government Y
−4	−28.82	Group Y riots in response to Government X's policies (property damage, 0 deaths)
−5	−32.12	Group Y riots in response to Government X's policies (property damage, 0 deaths)
−6	−60.18	Government X fires into crowd of Group X protesters (40 deaths)
−7	−63.65	Election violence in region Z between Government X and Group Y (100 deaths)
−8	−70.12	Government X suspends the national constitution. Population Y is affected
−9	−85.18	Group X violently topples President Y's government; X installs itself in power
−10	−90.71	Government X executes hundreds of members of Group Y

Source: adapted from Shellman (2004)

Table 4.2 Details of cooperation variables

Original value	Weight	Description
1	9.94	Group X praises Institution Y for policy implementation.
2	16.35	Government X promises Group Y that it will make concessions to end the dispute
3	25.88	Group X signs pact with Government Y. Pact promises to end a minor dispute between X and Y
4	27.71	Government X ends local curfew in Region Y
5	41.23	Government X agrees to allow regional elections to be held in Region Y
6	44.65	Government X ends the nationwide state of emergency. Population Y is affected
7	69.47	Government X allows opposition Group Y to take power following the election
8	73.94	Government X holds first national elections in 14 years (under old constitution). Population Y is allowed to participate

Table continued

Table 4.2 Continued

Original value	Weight	Description
9	77.17	Government Y implements new constitution that guarantees political and civil rights to Group X
10	84.06	Internal war between Group X and Government Y is terminated due to a resolution. Both X's and Y's needs are guaranteed

Source: adapted from Shellman (2004)

since violent forms of both repression and protest usually grow out of non-violent and less violent confrontation.

To account for the potentially very different dynamics between protest and repression under different institutional settings, I estimate the models separately for democratic, semi-democratic and autocratic regimes.[9] I create a number of sets from each country, so that, within a set, the Polity value from the Polity IVd dataset (Marshall and Jaggers 2001) is consistent. I collapse those sets of one country together where the Polity difference is of the value one.[10] Whenever the Polity variable changes by more than one value, it starts a new set for the analysis, using the exact day of the change. For example, in the case of Nigeria, the IPI data range from January 1983 to December 1992. The Polity variable takes on three different values between this time period, creating three subsets for Nigeria. The first one covers the time span from 1 January 1983 to 31 December 1983. During this time, the value of the Polity variable is seven, indicating the broadly democratic structure of the Second Republic under President Shagari. The second set ranges from 1 January 1984 to 3 May 1989, with the value of the Polity variable equal to minus seven. This represents the authoritarian rule of Generals Mohammed Buhari and Ibrahim Babangida. The third set covers the period from 4 May 1989 to the end of the dataset on 31 December 1992, also under Babangida. The value of the Polity variable during this time is minus five, indicating a semi-democracy that allowed for some participation and competition in the form of political parties. For every country, the cut-off points are based on the Polity scale, as described in the example for Nigeria. Table A.3 in the Appendix shows the sets, their labels, the time period over which each set spans, as well as the corresponding Polity value. Every country-set with a Polity value between seven and ten is labelled 'democracy', with the value between minus six and six 'semi-democracy', and 'autocracy' between minus seven and minus ten. The sample consists of six democracies, eight semi-democracies and four autocracies. Eleven sets are from Latin America and seven from Africa.

Figure 4.1 shows the level of protest, repression, dissident and state accommodation in an average month, plus some examples of the kinds of events represented by the numerical value. The graph shows that semi-

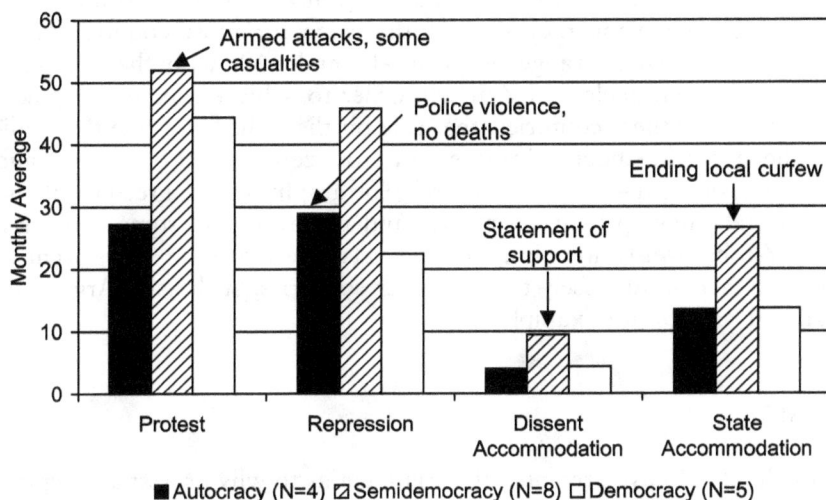

Figure 4.1 Average monthly values of coercion and accommodation.

Note: Colombia is excluded from this graph because of the high levels of protest and repression due to the conflict between the government and the drug cartel

Source: Carey (2006)

democracies experience the most intense events compared to democracies and autocracies. Autocracies seem to have been effective in preventing overt dissent, showing the lowest level of protest, while being less repressive than semi-democracies but more repressive than democracies. As expected, democracies have the lowest level of repression, but surprisingly both democracies and autocracies experience the same levels of dissident and state accommodation.

Figures A.4 to A.12 in the Appendix graphically show the development of protest, repression and democracy over time in each of the nine countries. There is one graph for each country. Due to data availability, the time periods covered for each country are not exactly identical, but the period ranges in general from the early 1980s to 1992. The exact month of the beginning and end of the analysed time period is listed in the titles of the figures. The graphs show the intensity of protest and repression, as well as the level of democracy[11] over time. The years are represented in the x-axis. For better graphical display, the data are monthly aggregated. For both protest and repression, I represent the total of conflict intensity in each month. The thin black line refers to the total intensity of protest, the thick black line refers to the total level of repression, and the horizontal line represents the degree of democracy. It should be noted that the scale on the y-axis on the left-hand side (intensity of protest and repression) is not consistent across all countries. For some countries the scale varies between zero and 1,200 (Mexico) and between zero and 5,000 for others (Colombia). The democracy scale is the same for most countries. It is plotted over its whole range between −10 and +10, with the exception of Colombia, Venezuela and Zaire. In order to achieve a better graphical presentation for these countries, the scale on the right-hand side that indicates the level of democracy ranges only from zero to +10 (Colombia and Venezuela), or from −10 to zero (Zaire). The graphs hint at a reciprocal and dynamic relationship between protest and repression. In some countries, like in Zimbabwe, Colombia and Venezuela, the two time series seem to move together more closely than in other countries, such as in Argentina, Brazil and Mexico, for example.

SUMMARY

In this chapter, I have presented the argument as to why protest and repression are interdependent and how they are expected to influence each other. The theoretical model put forward in this chapter focuses on the conflictual behaviour of government and non-government actors, and incorporates accommodation into the analysis of domestic conflict. I outlined why, and in what way, the interaction between the state and the opposition is influenced by the political regime of the country, taking into account the pacifying effect of institutionalized democracies. The final part of the chapter introduced the data on conflict and cooperation for selected African and Latin American countries, and showed how protest and repression have varied over time in these countries. The next chapter turns to the statistical analysis of the dynamic protest–repression nexus.

Notes

1 The analysis presented in this chapter is based on Carey (2006). I am grateful to Sage Publishing for permission to use the material in this book.
2 Moore (2000) comes to a similar conclusion by arguing that high levels of repression are usually followed by lower levels of repression, which effectively counterbalances the tendency for conflicts to spiral out of control.
3 This does not suggest that all physical acts are driven by clear and deliberate intent. But I would argue that non-physical behaviour, such as verbal statements or suggestions, is more likely to come out of impulse reactions compared to physical acts, such as participating in a demonstrations or preventing people from demonstrating.
4 See http://garnet.acns.fsu.edu/~whmoore/ipi/ipi.html for more details.
5 Using data drawn from news reports relies on the assumption that all events in question are reported with the same probability, or at least that there are no systematic errors in reporting news events. It is typically argued that it is in the interest of journalists not only to report events accurately, but also to report developments and activities 'evenly', meaning reporting all events that are of comparable importance and that are observable within their geographic area of focus. The IPI project utilizes four resources: Reuters North

American Service, Reuters World Service, the *New York Times* Index and the Africa Research Bulletin. Hence the IPI project makes use of a very large pool of resources, and increases the density and quality of the recorded events. In a study on the utility of Reuters in comparison to regional and local sources, Sommer and Scarritt (1999) found that Reuters has high face validity. Using data from Zambia–Zimbabwe interactions between 1982 and 1993, they also found that local news sources offered more dense coverage of physical environment and natural resource issue areas than did Reuters. However, Reuters' coverage was far superior in the political issue area. Since this study is interested in the political issue area, this shortcoming of Reuters in comparison to local news sources should be an advantage.

6 For a detailed discussion of this transformation, see Shellman (2004).

7 I also performed the analysis with quarterly aggregated data. This did not substantially alter the results.

8 This is consistent with the coding procedure applied for the general analysis presented in Chapter 3.

9 VARs are also based on the assumption that the relationships between the variables are stable across the time period. This is an unreasonable assumption for a country that undergoes a regime change, which is also shown by statistical stability tests.

10 Chile and Zaire differ from this rule due to autocorrelation in the errors.

11 The variable labelled 'Democracy' is the polity variable taken from Polity IV, which is calculated by subtracting the Autocracy score from the Democracy score, and ranges from −10 to +10.

5 Analysing domestic conflict and accommodation

To analyse the daily interactions of the repression–protest nexus I employ vector autoregression (VAR) (Freeman 1983; Freeman *et al.* 1989; Sims 1987).[1] VAR models can accommodate dynamics, specific concepts of causality and reciprocal relationships, and are therefore particularly well suited to the empirical investigation of the two-way relationship between protest and repression. The advantages of VAR models are that they are based on weak theoretical assumptions and that all variables are treated as endogenous. Hence, it does not have to be predetermined whether, and in what way, protest affects repression or, rather, whether repression affects protest in certain ways (Davis and Ward 1990). The researcher selects certain variables without having to specify the type and direction of the relationship between them. The goal of VARs is 'to find important interrelationships among the variables' (Enders 1995: 301). Although VAR models have been criticized for being atheoretical, the weak theoretical assumptions and the flexibility are an advantage in this context, bearing in mind the different and contradicting theories in this area of research.

Every endogenous variable in the VAR is regressed on a constant, its own lagged values and on the lagged values of all other endogenous variables in the system. Hence, the VAR models analysed here consist of four equations, since they include four variables:

$$
\begin{aligned}
\text{Protest}_t = \quad & c_1 + \beta_{111}\text{Protest}_{t-1} + \ldots + \beta_{11p}\text{Protest}_{t-p} + \\
& \beta_{121}\text{Repression}_{t-1} + \ldots + \beta_{12p}\text{Repression}_{t-p} + \\
& \beta_{131}\text{Dissident Accommodation}_{t-1} \\
& + \ldots + \beta_{13p}\text{Dissident Accommodation}_{t-p} + \\
& \beta_{141}\text{State Accommodation}_{t-1} \\
& + \ldots + \beta_{14p}\text{State Accommodation}_{t-p} + \varepsilon_1 \\
\text{Repression}_t = \quad & c_2 + \beta_{211}\text{Protest}_{t-1} + \ldots + \beta_{21p}\text{Protest}_{t-p} + \\
& \beta_{221}\text{Repression}_{t-1} + \ldots + \beta_{22p}\text{Repression}_{t-p} +
\end{aligned}
$$

β_{231}Dissident Accommodation$_{t\text{-}1}$
$+\ldots+ \beta_{23p}$Dissident Accommodation$_{t\text{-}p}$ +

β_{241}State Accommodation$_{t\text{-}1}$
$+\ldots+ \beta_{24p}$State Accommodation$_{t\text{-}p}$ + ε_2

Dissident Accommodation$_t$ =c_3 + β_{311}Protest$_{t\text{-}1}$ +$\ldots+ \beta_{31p}$Protest$_{t\text{-}p}$ +

β_{321}Repression$_{t\text{-}1}$ +$\ldots+ \beta_{32p}$Repression$_{t\text{-}p}$ +

β_{331}Dissident Accommodation$_{t\text{-}1}$
$+\ldots+ \beta_{33p}$Dissident Accommodation$_{t\text{-}p}$ +

β_{341}State Accommodation$_{t\text{-}1}$
$+\ldots+ \beta_{34p}$State Accommodation$_{t\text{-}p}$ + ε_3

State Accommodation$_t$ =c_4 + β_{411}Protest$_{t\text{-}1}$ +$\ldots+ \beta_{41p}$Protest$_{t\text{-}p}$ +

β_{421}Repression$_{t\text{-}1}$ +$\ldots+ \beta_{42p}$Repression$_{t\text{-}p}$ +

β_{431}Dissident Accommodation$_{t\text{-}1}$
$+\ldots+ \beta_{43p}$Dissident Accommodation$_{t\text{-}p}$ +

β_{441}State Accommodation$_{t\text{-}1}$
$+\ldots+ \beta_{44p}$State Accommodation$_{t\text{-}p}$ + ε_4

Each equation contains lags of the variables Protest, Repression, Dissident Accommodation and State Accommodation. For the statistical analysis, I use the natural log of all four variables due to their skewed distribution.[2] C is the constant and ε is the error term in each equation. The first subscript refers to the whole equation (such as the first equation, for example). The second subscript refers to a particular variable (such as Protest, for example) and the third subscript indicates the particular parameter of a variable (such as the parameter of the first lag of Protest, for example). P indicates the number of lags used in the VAR. The error terms are assumed to be uncorrelated white noise disturbances. The lag length p is determined separately for each set so that there is no significant autocorrelation in the error terms, and is specified using the Akaike and Schwartz criterion (Charemza and Deadman 1997; Enders 1995).[3] The lags vary for the different sets, with the average lag length being 8.7 days.

VAR models of interest are not the individual β coefficients, as in ordinary least squares regressions. The specific coefficients from specific lags have no substantive meaning. More important is whether all lags from one particular variable are *jointly* significantly different from zero. Hence, the underlying question is whether the history of one variable can improve the prediction of the dependent variable. This notion is based on the concept of Granger causality (Freeman 1983). The notion of Granger causality is that if a variable Y can be better predicted from past values of both X and Y than by past values of Y alone, then X Granger causes Y (Freeman 1983;

Granger 1969; Pierce 1977). For example, if the prediction of protest can be improved by using both the history of protest as well as the history of repression, then repression 'Granger causes' protest. In other words, if in a model with protest as the dependent variable and lagged values of protest on the right-hand side of the equation, lagged values of repression are jointly significantly different from zero, then repression can be said to 'Granger cause' protest.

In short, for the analysis I use 18 sets, estimating 18 different VAR models. In each model, every endogenous variable is regressed on a constant, its own lagged values and on the lagged values of all other endogenous variables in the system. F-tests are used to determine whether the inclusion of the lagged values increases the ability to predict the values of the variables on the left-hand side of the equation.

Table 5.1 summarizes the results of the F-tests based on the VAR models for the 18 sets.[4] The first line in the top row lists the dependent variable of the four regressions and the second line contains the initials of the independent variables, i.e. the lags of which are tested to improve the prediction of the dependent variable. Where the F-test of one variable was found to be statistically significant at a level of $p < 0.05$, it is noted with an 'X' in the table. The last row summarizes the results of the F-tests across all sets. The first line in the last row lists the total number of sets in which that particular variable was found to improve the prediction of the dependent variable. Below this are the corresponding percentages. The first column shows where each particular set is located on the Polity scale, which ranges from −10 (autocratic) to +10 (democratic).

To facilitate the comparison of the results across regime types, Table 5.2 summarizes the results over the three regime types. The first column lists the number of sets that fall in the respective regime category, showing that the sample contains six democratic sets, eight semi-democratic sets and four autocratic ones. The first row for each of the three regime categories refers to the number of sets in which a particular relationship was found and the second row refers to the sets in which this relationship was found as a percentage of the overall number of democratic, semi-democratic or autocratic sets respectively. For example, the first number six in the 'Protest' column means that in six democratic sets, protest was found to 'Granger cause' protest. The number 100 below indicates that this corresponds to 100 per cent of the democratic sets in the sample.

I argued in the previous chapter that protest follows repression and that repression follows protest. The results support this in the majority of cases. In two-thirds of the sets (67 per cent) repression leads to protest, whereas in 13 sets (72 per cent) protest leads to repression. Hostile behaviour from one actor is usually followed by hostile behaviour from the other. It has also been argued that, in democracies, protest is less likely to lead to repression due to institutional and normative constraints. Table 5.2 shows that protest leads to repression in five (of six) democracies, in five (of eight) semi-democracies

Table 5.1 Summary of F-tests

DV		Protest				Repression				Dissident accommodation				State accommodation			
Polity	Granger cause	P	R	DA	SA	P	R	DA	SA	P	R	DA	SA	P	R	DA	SA
−8	Argentina I	X			X		X		X	X	X		X		X	X	
7/8	Argentina II	X	X	X		X	X		X	X	X	X			X	X	X
−3	Brazil I	X	X		X	X	X								X		X
7/8	Brazil II	X	X			X		X									
−6	Chile I	X	X				X					X	X		X	X	X
−1	Chile II														X		
8	Chile III	X	X				X		X						X		
8/9	Colombia I	X				X	X		X			X					X
−3	Mexico I	X	X	X		X	X	X		X					X		
0	Mexico II	X	X	X		X		X		X							
9/8	Venezuela I	X	X		X	X	X	X	X	X				X	X	X	X
7	Nigeria I	X	X		X	X	X			X				X	X		
−7	Nigeria II	X		X		X	X	X						X	X		
−5	Nigeria III	X				X					X				X		
−9	Zaire I	X	X	X	X	X	X		X	X	X	X	X	X	X		X
−8	Zaire II	X	X	X	X	X	X		X	X	X	X		X	X	X	X
4/5	Zimbabwe I	X	X			X	X		X					X		X	X
1	Zimbabwe II	X					X										
	TOTAL (18)	17	12	6	6	13	14	5	8	8	5	5	4	6	13	6	8
	%	94	67	33	33	72	78	28	44	44	28	28	22	33	72	33	44

Note: X = F-test for the lags of this variable was statistically significant at $p<0.05$; DV = Dependent variable; P = Protest, R = Repression, DA = Dissident accommodation, SA = State accommodation.

Source: Carey (2006)

Table 5.2 Summary of F-tests by regime type

N	DV / Granger cause	Protest				Repression				Dissident accommodation				State accommodation			
		P	R	DA	SA	P	R	DA	SA	P	R	DA	SA	P	R	DA	SA
6	Democracy	6	5	2	2	5	4	2	5	2	1	2	1	2	4	1	4
	%	100	83	33	33	83	67	33	83	33	17	33	17	33	67	17	67
8	Semi-dem.	7	5	1	1	5	6	1	2	4	2	2	2	3	5	3	2
	%	86	63	13	13	63	75	13	25	50	25	25	25	38	63	38	25
4	Autocracy	4	2	3	3	3	4	2	1	2	2	1	1	1	4	2	2
	%	100	50	75	75	75	100	50	25	50	50	25	25	25	100	50	50

Note: The numbers in the cells refer to the number of sets for which the lags of the variable had an statistically significant F-test at $p < 0.05$.

DV = Dependent variable, N = Total number of cases in this category, P = Protest, R = Repression, DA = Dissident accommodation, SA = State accommodation and three (of four) autocracies. Although the difference between regime types is not particularly large, the hypothesis about the effect of regime type on the impact of protest on repression cannot be confirmed.

Regime type was also expected to influence the effect of repression on protest. Democracies were argued to be more prone to experiencing protest as a response to repression, while such a link was hypothesized to be absent in autocracies. Of the 12 sets where repression was found to lead to protest (two-thirds of the total sample), five are democracies (of the total of six democracies), five semi-democracies (out of eight) and two autocracies (out of four). Hence, repression leads to protest in all but one of the democracies but in only half of the autocracies, lending some support to the hypotheses on the role of regime type in the repression–protest link. Citizens in democracies generally resist hostile government behaviour by participating in actions of dissent.

Note that in nine of the thirteen sets where protest leads to repression, repression also leads to protest. In most cases where the state retaliates against dissent, the government can expect the population to respond with further protest. This suggests that repression is not a very useful instrument for making a protesting opposition cooperate. Indeed, in only five of the eighteen sets (28 per cent), repression leads to dissident accommodation. Those five sets consist of only one democracy (of six democracies, i.e. 17 per cent), but include two of the four autocracies. Particularly in democracies, hostile government behaviour seems to be ineffective in soliciting accommodation from the opposition. In autocracies, repression is a more successful tool for getting the opposition to accommodate the government. This suggests that, in autocracies, the opposition does not pursue a hard line against the government in the face of repression because it is too dangerous. However, in a democracy the opposition appears to be more confident in not giving in to the regime, even in the face of hostile government actions. It can be speculated that, in such regimes, the opposition is more confident that negative state sanctions will not escalate so that the benefits of not cooperating with a hostile government outweigh the costs of pursuing a hard line.

Protest is similarly ineffective for getting the government to accommodate the opposition. Protest leads to accommodating behaviour of the government in only one third of the analyses, without significant differences between the regime types. Government accommodation, on the other hand, was expected to lead to protest since an accommodating government can be perceived as increasing the benefits, and lowering the costs, of dissent. This hypothesis is supported in only one-third of the sets. Most of those are autocracies (three out of four autocracies). In autocracies, if a government accommodates the opposition, then this is likely to be interpreted as a weakness that is exploited by the opposition.

Stronger support is found for the argument that dissident accommodation is not exploited by the government with repression. In only five of the eighteen sets (28 per cent), dissident accommodation 'Granger causes' repression. Hence, the hypothesis is supported by over two-thirds of the cases. When faced with a cooperating opposition, the domestic (in the form of backlash) and international (in the form of shaming and potential loss of trade) costs of repression generally outweigh the benefits. Note that two of the cases where repression follows dissident accommodation are autocracies (50 per cent of the autocratic sets). Not surprisingly, autocracies seem to be less worried than other regime types about the costs of repression in response to dissident accommodation.

Finally, the analysis tested the arguments that both protest and repression continue once they have been initiated, and that accommodating behaviour is persistent in democracies but not in autocracies. The most consistent finding across all sets of analysis is that protest is highly autoregressive. This result is found in all but one of the VAR analyses. This supports the argument that it is most difficult to initiate a protest movement, but less costly to sustain it once the rebels have overcome the dilemma of collective action. These findings are in line with the results from the ordered probit analysis presented in Chapter 3, which also showed that domestic protest in one year increases the probability of protest in the following year. The result lends support to models of collective action and their implication for organizing dissent. Rational actors approaches, such as the threshold model, the bandwagon model and the micromobilization model, argue that it is most difficult to initiate a protest movement. Once a certain threshold of dissent organization has been overcome, it is less costly to sustain that movement once the rebels have overcome the dilemma of collective action (Oberschall 1994; Rasler 1996; Tarrow 1994). It is more costly to initiate protest, since the costs of participating are high and the benefits seem low when only a few people engage in the protest activity. But once a certain threshold has been crossed, the costs of participation decline and the perceived benefits increase. Unfortunately, this threshold is never clearly specified. Hence, the argument that is tested within this framework is not the threshold per se, but whether protest is likely to continue once it has been initiated.

Repression is found to be autoregressive in 14 sets (78 per cent). Once the government begins to violate the rights of its citizens, it is likely to continue to do so. Again, the same results were found with the yearly data and the different statistical methodology presented in the previous chapter. The rationale behind the autoregressiveness of repression is institutional inertia. Once the government establishes a security and repressive apparatus, this apparatus is likely to stay in place. Repressive institutions have a self-perpetuating effect, but there are interesting differences between regime types. Whereas repression is autoregressive in all autocracies, only four democracies (67 per cent of democracies) and six semi-democracies (75 per cent of semi-democracies) exhibit this pattern. Democratic norms and institutions seem to have a dampening effect on institutional inertia when the government shows hostile behaviour towards the opposition. But no such constraints are in place in autocracies.

In general, conflictual behaviour (protest and repression) is much more often found to have a sustained and consistent pattern compared to accommodating behaviour (dissident accommodation and state accommodation). Across the countries, dissident accommodation appears to be more sporadic than any other behaviour. It is found to be autoregressive in only five of the eighteen sets, compared to eight for state accommodation. There are small differences between regime types: state accommodation is autoregressive in two-thirds of democracies, whereas the same result is found in only half of the autocracies and a quarter of the semi-democracies. The inconsistency of institutional rules and roles in semi-democracies might lead to such sporadic behaviour of the government, since it probably does not want to risk losing too much ground by consistently accommodating the opposition. Overall, accommodating behaviour plays a rather minor role in the interaction between the government and the population. It does not seem to have a strong or consistent effect on domestic conflict. This might be influenced by the data-generating process, due to potential under-reporting of accommodating behaviour. One could argue that journalists are likely to focus more on reporting conflict and confrontation than accommodation.

Table 5.3 summarizes the results from the 18 different VAR models by region. The first column shows that the analysis included eleven sets from Latin America and seven from Africa. The results reveal three main differences between the two regions. First, repression is more likely to continue, once it has been started, in Africa than in Latin America. In all seven African sets repression was found to be autoregressive, whereas the same relationship was found in only seven of the eleven (64 per cent) in the Latin American sample. Second, protest is met with repression in all but one African set, whereas protest leads to repression in only seven of the eleven Latin American sets (64 per cent). The finding that protest in African countries is usually met with force from the government is also supported by other studies (Bratton and van de Walle 1992; Wiseman 1986). One possible explanation for this finding might be that governments in Africa are relatively weak compared to their Latin American counterparts. They are ruled by the utilization of neopatrimonial relationships (Bratton and van de Walle 1994) and do not rely on well-developed institutions and bureaucracy. Additionally, they generally have fewer resources at their disposal to rule countries whose geography, distribution of populations and lack of infrastructure make gaining and keeping control over their constituencies particularly difficult (Herbst 2000). These characteristics are likely to make governments even more susceptible to threats, and therefore more likely to respond by intimidating and repressing opposition groups and potential rebels.

The third main difference between the two regions is that although repression has been found to be generally a poor tool in pushing the opposition into accommodating actions, this strategy seems to be particularly unsuccessful in Latin America. In only two of the eleven Latin American sets

Table 5.3 Summary of F-tests by region

	DV	Protest				Repression				Dissident accommodation				State accommodation			
N	Granger cause	P	R	DA	SA	P	R	DA	SA	P	R	DA	SA	P	R	DA	SA
11	LA	10	7	3	3	7	7	3	5	5	2	3	2	3	7	4	5
	%	91	64	27	27	64	64	27	45	45	18	27	18	27	64	36	45
7	Africa	7	5	3	3	6	7	2	3	3	3	2	2	3	6	2	3
	%	100	71	43	43	86	100	29	43	43	43	29	29	43	86	29	43

Note: The numbers in the cells refer to the number of sets for which the lags of the variable had an statistically significant F-test at $p < 0.05$.
DV = Dependent variable, N = Total number of cases in this category, P = Protest, R = Repression, DA = Dissident accommodation, SA = State accommodation

did dissident accommodation follow repression (18 per cent), while the comparable figures for Africa are three out of seven (43 per cent). This could be due to the nature of opposition groups in Latin America compared to those in Africa. In Latin America, protest movements against ruling elites have often been driven by organized groups. For example, labour unions and churches have played important roles in opposition governments in Latin America. In Africa, dissent has primarily been driven by more spontaneous activities, by students and teachers, rather than by labour unions or business organizations, partly because of the weak and under-developed middle class compared to that in Latin America.[5] State pressure is likely to be less effective in pushing an opposition into cooperative behaviour that is based on an organized network than an opposition that is mainly made up of spontaneously grouped-together individuals, which might be united in opposing the government, but otherwise represents a diverse selection of society.

SUMMARY

In this chapter, I have presented the results of an analysis that investigated the interaction between domestic conflict and accommodation, focusing on dynamics and reciprocity, using data from African and Latin American countries between the late 1970s and early 1990s.

Overall, the results from these time-series analyses supported the findings from the macro-level analyses presented in Chapter 3. Conflictual behaviour by one actor leads to conflictual behaviour by the other. Once such behaviour has been initiated, it is likely to continue. Figure 5.1 summarizes the results of the 18 vector autoregression models. The arrows show the relationship for which support has been found in the majority of the 18 separate analyses. The boxes around protest and repression indicate that both have consistently been found to continue over time, while accommodating

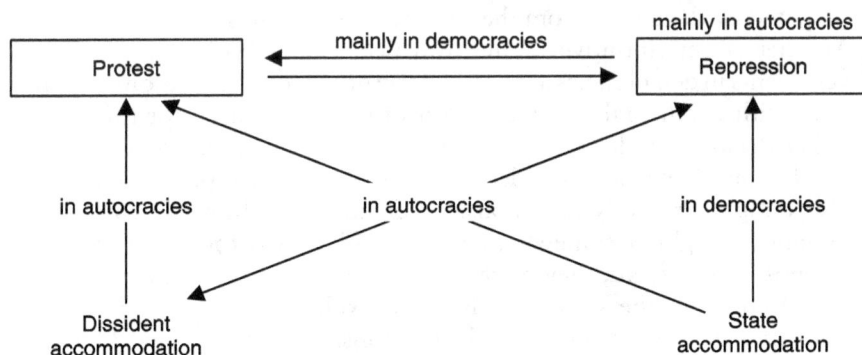

Figure 5.1 Summary of VAR results.

behaviour, both from the government and the opposition, appears to be more sporadic and short-lived. The time-series analysis of the individual countries confirms the results from the Chapter 3. Once the start-up costs of initiating protest and repression have been overcome, these actions are likely to continue. But consistent repressive behaviour is more likely to be found in autocracies than in democracies or semi-democracies. Once autocratic rulers have decided to intimidate the opposition, they are highly likely to do so, while governments in democracies appear to be more willing and able to switch back to alternative strategies.

The VAR results also confirm that protest leads to repression and repression leads to protest. But looking at the results more closely reveals that only 50 per cent of the sets show an interdependent dynamic, where protest causes repression *and* repression causes protest at the same time. This reciprocity is found overwhelmingly in democracies (five out of six, but in only two out of eight semi-democracies and in two out of four autocracies). This is due to the finding that it is mostly in democracies that repression leads to protest. This is consistent with the argument put forward earlier: I argued that, compared to non-democracies, in democracies people were less likely to put up with repression; instead, they were expected to take action against such government behaviour. There is some support for this argument, as in all but one democratic set protest follows repression, while this is the case in only half the autocratic sets and in five out of eight semi-democracies. In democratic regimes, people seem to have certain expectations about the behaviour of their governments and are unlikely to put up with actions that violate the rights of citizens.

Due to democratic norms and institutional constraints, protest was expected to be less likely to lead to repression in democracies than in other regimes. The results, however, do not support this expectation. Protest leads to repression in all but one of the democratic sets analysed above. This shows that even democracies are not particularly tolerant of dissent, although the response of the government is likely to be less violent than in non-democracies, as hinted at by the summary statistics shown in Figure 4.1 and highlighted by the results from the ordered probit analysis.

Another counterintuitive finding revealed by the VAR analyses is that governments in democracies are particularly prone to follow accommodating actions with conflictual behaviour. Part of the explanation for this finding could be the kinds of democracies that are present in the sample. Apart from Colombia and Venezuela, the democratic sets in the sample represent relatively young, or recently re-established, democracies. In such democracies, governments might be somewhat hesitant to give away too much ground to the opposition. Instead, they might focus on establishing themselves as the main authority in the system. This could explain why in the democratic regime in Argentina under President Alfonsín, which followed military rule, and in Chile under President Aylwin after the end of General Pinochet's rule, state accommodation was followed by repressive actions. But this behaviour was also found in Colombia and Venezuela. Colombia is an outlier case because of the intense and protracted conflict between the government and the drug cartel, which could explain why the government has been quick to use conflictual behaviour after accommodating its opponents. With respect to Venezuela, it is worth noting that the level of repression has been comparatively low. At the same time, the country suffered from a deteriorating economy, which resulted in violent riots in 1989 (Myers 1996). Being faced with intense forms of dissent might explain why the government often used confrontation and coercion after accommodating the opposition.

While in democracies accommodating actions have often led to repression, in autocracies protest has generally led to protest. This suggests that, in autocracies, the opposition is hesitant in giving away too much ground and chooses to pursue its interests by confronting the government while at the same time showing accommodating behaviours. It is interesting to note that in all but one instance where dissident accommodation led to repression, dissident accommodation was followed by protest. Although this is just speculative given the nature of the analysis, this result might suggest that the opposition switches from accommodating to conflictual behaviour when its accommodating behaviour is met with repression by the government.

Figure 5.1 also highlights that, in autocracies, accommodating actions are likely to be viewed by the other side as a weakness and are exploited by responding with conflictual behaviour. Although in only few cases state accommodation led to protest and dissident accommodation to repression, if it did, it was usually in a autocratic regime. When institutions that facilitate peaceful bargaining, inclusion of different groups and compromise are missing, accommodating behaviour by one actor is likely to be exploited by the other side.

What becomes particularly noticeable in this graph is that while the models perform well in explaining conflictual behaviour, the same cannot be said for the accommodating actions of the government and the opposition. The overall lack of consistent explanations for cooperative behaviour could partly be due to the nature of the data-generating process. This is based on coding news sources, where conflictual behaviour potentially receives more news coverage than cooperative actions. But I would argue that there is another factor that contributes to conflict being better supported by the empirical findings than cooperation. Most of our theories and hypotheses, including the ones presented in this book, focus on understanding and explaining conflictual behaviour. Large amounts of research have addressed questions of why governments abuse the rights of their citizens (e.g. Poe and Tate 1994), why rebels torture civilians (e.g. Weinstein 2007) or why civilians kill each other (e.g. Kalyvas 2006), yet little attention has been given to understanding why disagreements do not lead to conflict and violence, why governments choose alternative strategies to deal with opposition, and why discontented groups do not take up arms against their government and fellow citizens. In short, more work is needed to find out why we observe peace and cooperation in situations where we would expect to see conflict and violence.

Notes

1 For another application of VAR in analysing reciprocity, see Davis and Ward (1990) and Moore (1995), but also Goldstein *et al.* (2001) and Enders and Sandler (1993) for the use of VAR in analysing anti-terrorism policies.
2 Since the natural log cannot be taken of zero, I add 0.5 to every variable based on $\ln(x)$ $\ln(x + 0.5)$.
3 In vector autoregression, as in other time-series models, it is assumed that the variables are stationary. If statistical tests, such as the augmented Dickey–Fuller test, show the presence of unit root, then it is usually recommended to difference the variables (Enders 1995). Although others argue that, in the context of VARs, variables should not be differenced because the goal is to determine the inter-relationships among the variables and not parameter estimates, therefore differencing would only lose information (Sims 1980). However, the analysis of the four variables used in my model shows that they are stationary. Also all VARs have been tested to be covariance-stationary (Hamilton 1994).
4 The detailed results for each case of the analysis can be obtained from the author upon request.
5 The characteristics of opposition groups are analysed in more detail in the case studies presented in Chapter 6.

6 Illustrative case studies: Chile and Nigeria

This chapter illustrates how the protest–repression nexus has played out in two countries: Chile and Nigeria. These micro-level investigations outline how the dynamics that were investigated using statistical approaches in the previous chapters developed under specific historical, cultural, economic and political conditions. The Chilean case study concentrates on the Pinochet regime from 1973–88 and the beginning of the subsequent democratic regime. The case study on Nigeria analyses the protest–repression nexus from the end of the Second Republic in 1983 to the return to civilian rule under Obasanjo in 1999. The two case studies were chosen from the sample of nine countries from Chapters 4 and 5 in order to represent the two regions, Latin America and Africa, and to provide variation in regime type to allow for the analysis of domestic conflict in different institutional settings.

CHILE: SOCIAL MOVEMENTS AND PROTEST UNDER PINOCHET

This section shows how the organized opposition, and the population at large, reacted to repression by the military regime under General Pinochet, and how Pinochet reacted to the behaviour of the masses. The case study focuses primarily on the time period from the military coup on 11 August 1973 to the plebiscite on 5 October 1988, in which General Pinochet was denied a second eight-year term as president. This qualitative analysis focuses on how the government and its opponents interacted with each other, and how they modified their strategies and behaviours based on their opponent's actions.

From the coup d'état to the rise of the social movement, 1973–83

As soon as the military junta toppled President Allende in August 1973, the new rulers initiated a widespread campaign of violence and state terror. This campaign was very effective in eliminating almost all forms of open resistance to the new regime and its repressive rulers. Immediately after the coup, 'the intensity of the repression was extremely high, and it was applied capriciously, since the armed forces did not know who their targets were' (Frühling 1984: 352). Rape, torture, disappearances and killings were widely used by all branches of the military. The regime's victims included members and sympathizers of the deposed government, labour organizers, university students, members of left-wing parties, as well as victims of political and personal vendettas (Commission of Truth and Reconciliation 1991: 25). According to Schneider, '1,261 civilians were executed between September and December of 1973' (1995: 78). In addition to these severe and widespread violations of life integrity rights, the military regime also curbed civil and political rights. Pinochet declared a state of siege, left-wing political parties were banned and all others suspended. Union elections were prohibited and police authorization was required for all public meetings and assemblies. These 'policies were designed to provoke intense fear and helplessness, not only among left-wing activists, but among the poor and working class as a whole' (Schneider 1995: 80).

After the initial surge of repression, which was largely uncoordinated and often erratic, General Pinochet created the Directorate of National Intelligence (Dirección Nacional de Inteligencia, DINA) in June 1974. The DINA was the Chilean secret police, headed by Pinochet's personal friend, General Manuel Contreras. DINA was separate from the Army. It centralized 'the intelligence gathering process and ... executed repressive policies in one specialized agency ... [to] diminish the costs involved in the repressive process ... and distinguished more clearly which targets were really dangerous' (Frühling 1984: 360). Repression became more selective and more secretive, which resulted in increasing numbers of disappearances, mainly of underground left-wing party members; these were largely university students (Frühling 1984; Oxhorn 1995). By mid-1975, between 40,000 and 50,000 civilians had been detained, and many of them brutally tortured (Schneider 1995: 3). The goal of DINA's strategy was to destroy left-wing parties (Schneider 1995: 85). DINA became immensely powerful:

> It commanded an empire of thousands and counted on the active collaboration of both civil and state enterprises such as the national telephone company, the national railroad, the merchant marine, the national airline, the Ministry of Foreign Affairs, and foreign diplomats.
> (Schneider 1995: 89)

In 1977, DINA was dissolved, in part because of pressure from the United States, and was replaced by the National Information Center (Centro Nacional de Información, CNI). With the creation of CNI, repression was further institutionalized and legalized under the authoritarian rule of law (Frühling 1984).

Pinochet's strategy of spreading fear and intimidation, and eliminating leaders of opposition groups paid off. The period between 1973 and 1983 was characterized by an almost complete absence of organized public dissent. Dissent was limited to defensive protests, such as hunger strikes against human rights violations (Garretón 2001). Dissent activities shared four features during this time period. First, protests were 'isolated incidents, erratic, and generally brief in duration. The size, irregularity, and brevity of the demonstrations reflected people's fears of government reprisals' (Garretón 2001: 266). Second, protest was not driven by the expectation to achieve a change in the system, but was instead a tool for opposition leaders to assert themselves. Third, opposition to the regime occurred under the institutional protection of the Catholic Church, which openly criticized Pinochet's repressive strategies. Finally, the leaders of the opposition were more radicalized than their members (Garretón 2001).

The rise and fall of mass protests, 1983–8

This domination of the military, and its effective repression of dissent and opposition, began to change during the early 1980s. Social movements began to re-emerge during the early 1980s. This culminated in a national day of protest on 11 May 1983 and led to a widespread mobilization campaign. The reason for this reawakening of the opposition was a change in the political opportunity structure (Hipsher 1996). The economic crisis at that time, combined with 'strong external support of civil protest by all of the opposition political parties and the Catholic Church' (Hipsher 1996: 281), created divisions within the government coalition, which, in turn, created the space and the political opportunity for organized opposition. The severe recession that hit Chile between 1981 and 1983 was not the first economic crisis under Pinochet. The reason the earlier recession, during 1975 and 1976, did not lead to organized protest was 'because no organization could survive. The left-wing parties were in retreat, the popular organizations destroyed, labor unions had been eliminated by the collapse of the industry, and the government was cohesive and strong' (Schneider 1995: 94). The political opportunity structure did not change because the recession in the mid-1970s did not weaken the government. In the early 1980s, the economic crisis led to a political crisis by dividing the military. At the same time, external support for protest grew, in the form of protection of shantytown movements by the Catholic Church. Finally, centrist political parties moved towards supporting the opposition movement (Hipsher 1998).

Chile's Copper Workers' Confederation (Confederación de Trabajadores del Cobre, CTC), which was the most influential labour union because of the country's dependency on copper exports, called for a national day of protest against the Pinochet dictatorship on 11 May 1983. The CTC was joined by several political parties and associations. The result was widespread protest in which large sectors of the population participated. These protests were repeated on a nearly monthly basis until 1987, 'fueling one of the most intense cycles of protest in Latin America in the 1980s' (Hipsher 1998: 150). The protest movement also included middle-class professionals, who stayed at home from work and kept their children at home from school. Women in middle-class areas banged their pots and pans in protest at the regime. University students and shantytown dwellers represented a particularly large proportion of the protesters (Schneider 1995). These protests could successfully be mobilized for the following reasons. They involved Chile's most powerful union (the CTC), they stressed broadly based defiance, which enabled multi-class participation, and the lower classes felt 'protected' by the middle classes, since Pinochet was more hesitant to use violence against these groups (Garretón 2001).

On 11 August 1983, the fourth opposition protest took place. This protest was 'met with the harshest repression to date. Eighteen thousand soldiers hit the streets of Santiago, treating the *poblaciones* with particular violence, killing twenty-six people and leaving hundreds wounded' (Huneeus 2007: 373). On 30 August 1983, the Canadian newspaper the *Globe and Mail* printed the following report:

> Major monthly protests against Gen. Pinochet's regime began in May and have increased in strength every month, in spite of curfews and growing repression. When 18,000 soldiers occupied Santiago, the capital, for this month's protest, more than 30 people were killed and more than 100 injured. Reports of severe brutality on the part of armed forces personnel and police sent a wave of horror and consternation through the country.

Protest led to repression, repression led to further protest, which further increased state violence. Despite state coercion and significant intimidation, in September of the same year, 'shantytown dwellers . . . staged the largest illegal land seizure in the country's history' (Hipsher 1996: 281), which involved 8,000 families on the outskirts of Santiago. The regime reacted with severe repression and arrests by the policy and armed forces.

The protests temporarily declined when the government imposed a state of siege in November 1984. But when this was lifted in August 1985, the protests resumed with even greater intensity. At the same time, the number of arrests rose steadily from 1,213 in 1982 to 4,537 in 1983, and up to 7,019 in 1986 (Arriagada 1988: 63). Using widespread coercion, the government tried to end the cycle of dissent by further increasing the costs of participating in the collective protest. Beginning in 1985, protests became less frequent. At the same time, dissent became more violent as the profile of the protesters changed. During 1985–6, members of the middle classes were less willing to mobilize due to a mix of government repression and concessions. Severe repression of the CTC made it harder for labour groups to mobilize, which meant that shantytown dwellers and students became the two dominant groups in the protest movements (Hipsher 1998). These two groups pursued more radical strategies, and used violent and confrontational tactics. National days of protest were replaced by demonstrations and armed attacks (Salazar 1990, cited in Hipsher 1998: 161).

In April 1986, the Democratic Alliance (Alianza Democrática, AD), a coalition that united moderate political opposition parties, and the Democratic Popular Movement (Movimiento Democrático Popular, MDP), which united left-wing parties and movements, formed the Assembly of Civil Society (Asamblea de la Civilidad, AC). The AC called for Pinochet's resignation and free and fair elections. It threatened a national strike if the regime did not respond positively within 30 days. Pinochet rejected the proposal, and the mobilization campaign peaked in a general strike on 2–3 July 1986, which 'managed to paralyze activities in Santiago for forty-eight hours' (Hipsher 1998: 161). This strike was met by a particularly harsh response from the government. During those two days, ten people were killed by government forces and two teenagers set on fire, which increased international attention to the human rights situation in Chile (Hipsher 1996; Schneider 1995).

After this general strike, the cycle of protest declined. This decline can be attributed to two related factors: the break between the Christian Democratic-led and the Communist-led opposition groups, and increased repression. The split in the opposition was caused by the escalation of left-wing violence, which alienated moderate groups in the opposition. Two incidents exemplified this escalation of violence. First, on 12 August 1986, it was discovered that a clandestine arsenal of weapons had been brought into the country by the Manuel Rodriguez Patriotic Front (Frente Patriótico Manuel Rodríguez, FPMR), the armed wing of the Chilean Communist Party (Partido Comunista de Chile, PCCH). Second, on 7 September of the same year, the FPMR carried out a failed assassination attempt on Pinochet, which led to another state of siege that lasted until early January 1987. These violent and extreme tactics were rejected by moderate opposition groups and most sections of the population. The centrist groups broke away from the left-wing groups and accepted the dictatorship's offer of negotiation. The purpose that the two groups attached to protest had started to diverge. The left-wing parties saw the purpose of dissent in paralysing and eventually overthrowing the military regime and used particularly violent tactics to this end. The centrist parties, however, viewed dissent as a tool for bringing the dictatorship to the negotiating table, and employed mainly non-violent strategies.

The second reason for the decline of protest was increasing state coercion. The cost of protest became so high that the majority preferred institutionalized forms of dissent over confrontational tactics (Hipsher 1998; Schneider 1995):

> Once opposition forces made the choice to purse a negotiated route to democracy social movement mobilization became increasingly rare. In

an attempt to ensure that the transition to democracy succeeded and was not thwarted by provocative violence, opposition parties of the center and center-left discouraged protest by movements and encouraged them to get involved in the Campaign for the 'no' and to work through the proper institutional channels.

(Hipsher 1998: 162)

In 1987, AD accepted the framework for the transition that had been laid out in the 1980 constitution. The strong links between the social movement and political parties meant that once the parties rejected mobilization in favour of limited democracy, movement leaders began to oppose active dissent and protest as well. Even shantytown dwellers, which had been one of the core groups in the protest movement, 'accepted that a limited democracy, constrained by the institutional and juridical legacies of Pinochet, was better than no democracy at all' (Hipsher 1996: 283). State coercion had effectively intimidated and split the opposition. Combined with the violent tactics of the Communist Party, which was rejected by large parts of the population, the opposition became divided, and the moderate groups entered negations with the government. Once negotiations had been made possible, the majority of the opposition did not want to jeopardize this process and preferred to accept the democratization timeline given by Pinochet than to continue to suffer under his dictatorship. As a result, the period of social movement and widespread dissent came to an end.

The politics of *apertura*

As outlined above, Pinochet responded harshly to nationwide strikes and demonstrations. But repression and coercion were not the only tactics that the military junta employed to deal with the opposition. Starting in 1983, repression was accompanied by a political strategy to quell the protest. On 15 December 1983, the *Washington Post* reported that '[g]overnment officials . . . believed a move towards liberalization could defuse the protest movement and channel unrest into a slow, controlled move toward democracy'. Huneeus argues that '[t]he military thought it important that the government recover the political initiative and apply measures to halt workers' protest, without relying solely on coercion, since they considered its costs too high' (2007: 372). Part of this strategy was a reshuffle of the Cabinet to incorporate more experienced civilian politicians. On 10 August 1983, a new cabinet was sworn in. Part of this new cabinet was a new interior minister, Sergio Onofre Jarpa. Jarpa had been elected senator for Santiago in March 1973 and was an experienced politician. He started a process of *apertura*. But Pinochet did not share these ideas of *apertura* with his interior minister and therefore limited Jarpa's influence (Huneeus 2007).

Jarpa started some initiatives as part of *apertura*, which had an important influence on the process that followed. He allowed leading politicians to return from exile and suspended media censorship for a while. This 'increased the amount and quality of political information in circulation, encouraging mobilization. Opposition parties found that they had more room to man-oeuvre as the political recess maintained since 1973 began to lose its edge' (Huneeus 2007: 372). Jarpa also met with some opposition leaders and, although the meetings were unsuccessful, they increased the visibility of these individuals. The interior minister also reinstated the right of interest groups to elect their own leaders. As a consequence, over the following two years, opposition leaders, who had been active politicians before the coup in 1973, won the elections of the main professional and student associations.

Pinochet undermined the politics of *apertura* by appointing parallel advisers. He 'continued his confrontational style with the opposition, because he thought the new stance had gone too far in helping his enemies' (Huneeus 2007: 380). In early 1985, Jarpa was removed from government. Huneeus summarizes the result of *apertura* as follows:

> The suspension of the apertura proved unable to turn back the clock and eliminate the new waves of political action that arose with the plurality of media, the politicization of interest groups, and parties' more active leadership. Independently of General Pinochet's decisions, the political system had changed, but this did not fully register with him.
> (Huneeus 2007: 382)

The politics of *apertura* not only allowed more space for the opposition: the repressive tactics of the regime, which now made their way into the more open media reporting, also divided 'proregime groups, who took different stands on Pinochet's succession and turned to the constitution to change the regime by defeating Pinochet in the 1988 plebiscite' (Huneeus 2007: 386). Hence, in the second half of the 1980s, the severity of repression and of the violent opposition tactics, combined with the effect of *apertura*, had strengthened moderates on both sides, who focused on changing the regime within the institutional constraints given by the 1980 constitution.

Summarizing the dynamics

Chile's history under Pinochet from 1973–88 highlights some of the main findings of the quantitative analyses presented earlier. It draws attention to how the dynamics between a repressive regime and its opponents can play out, and which factors influence the nature of these dynamics. It showed that when governments feel particularly threatened, they will employ repression to minimize the threat and to increase their own strength. And, in the presence of widespread repression, people can be mobilized to participate in active protest against the regime only when certain conditions are in place. Immediately after the coup, the new military rulers were particularly vulnerable because of the potential influence of the previous regime and its supporters, and therefore particularly receptive to threat. As a result, the military junta employed severe coercion to eliminate any opposition, to instil fear and intimidation into the population, to secure the new regime and to increase its strength. This behaviour was facilitated by the fact that large sectors of society, in particular the middle classes, had been disillusioned by the Allende regime and welcomed the coup. The repression silenced and immobilized organized social movements and successfully intimidated the population. During this early time period of severe coercion, the opposition concentrated on defensive protests against human rights violations instead of seeking confrontation with the military regime. The limited and isolated dissent activities were facilitated by the institutional protection of the Catholic Church.

The fate of the opposition movement improved with a change in the political opportunity structure, which was facilitated by the economic crisis during the early 1980s. This crisis divided the military and thus weakened the government. At the same time, the Catholic Church increased its protection of shantytown movements, while centrist parties moved to support the opposition movement. A combination of a weakened government and a united and broad opposition resulted in mass protests. These protests were possible because of Chile's long tradition of strong political parties and unions, which were able to mobilize large sectors of the population. As highlighted by the quantitative analysis, this widespread dissent led to more widespread and violent repression, starting a vicious circle of violence, where the response of the organized opposition became more violent and, in turn, the regime became more repressive.

These developments show that protest and repression often accelerate each other, but that they cannot spiral upwards indefinitely. The severity of violence laid the ground for its own decline. The high levels of state violence were increasingly rejected by pro-government groups and international actors, while the violent dissent tactics split and weakened the opposition. Oxhorn argues that '[p]opular mobilization becomes potentially threatening because it may engender a backlash by hardliners within the authoritarian regime. Political parties become agents for moderation and social control to ensure that the transition runs its course' (1994: 50). Combined with the effect of *apertura*, moderates within and outside the government now focused on changing the military regime within the given constitutional limits. As a result, the active social movement was replaced with negotiations, concentrating on voting against another eight-year term for General Pinochet in the 1988 plebiscite. With increasing democratization, dissent activities outside of institutionalized channels were rejected by all parties. Protest and dissent – for example, in the form of illegal land seizures by the homeless – were rejected and condemned from all sides after the elections in December 1989, arguing that this sort of behaviour could not be tolerated in a democracy (Hipsher 1996). While the strength of political parties and associations, and their link to civil society, facilitated the mobilization of mass protests a few years earlier, those same characteristics contributed to the decline of the social movement under a more democratic institutional setting.

NIGERIA: THE DOMINATION OF REPRESSION OVER PROTEST

The relationship between the government and civil society in Nigeria is marked by very different characteristics compared to those in Chile. In Nigeria, interactions between the government and the opposition, or civil society at large, have been dominated by the long and pervasive military rule, which lasted for almost 30 years.[1] Decades of repressive military rule, combined with severe economic crises and poverty, significantly influenced the power balance in favour of the regime, and to the detriment of the opposition and civil society. In this section, I highlight the main character-istics of the government and the opposition, which shaped the interaction between these groups from the end of the Second Republic in 1983 up to the Fourth Republic, which started with the election of the civilian President Obasanjo in 1999.

Suppressed civil society under Buhari and Babangida, 1983–93

The Second Republic under President Shagari was short-lived. The inability of Shagari to address severe poverty and to deal with the economic crisis, together with being blamed for corruption and mismanagement, led to a bloodless coup by Major-General Muhammad Buhari on 31 December 1983. Buhari's regime was the most authoritarian and repressive the country had seen, launching the 'War Against Indiscipline'. He issued a large number of decrees, which facilitated his particularly heavy-handed approach. The decrees allowed the military junta to detain persons for three months with-out charge (Decree 2), to jail journalists for 'false accusations' (Decree 4), and placed the government above and outside the law (Decree 13) (Aiyede 2003). This resulted in a public outcry, which, combined with the continu-ously declining economy, facilitated another bloodless coup, by Major-General Ibrahim Babangida, on 27 August 1985. After Babangida took power, he promised to end human rights abuses. He 'began with a pretence at openness and respect for human rights in an apparent move to win public support' (Aiyede 2003: 8). For example, he legalized labour unions and professional associations that had been banned under Buhari.

At the same time, from the mid-1980s, civil society, which had effectively been suppressed under Buhari, grew stronger. The continuing economic crisis and the weakness of the state, which manifested itself in corrup-tion and the abuse of power, undermined the legitimacy of the military government. This, in turn, strengthened civil society. Additionally, debates about IMF loans in 1985 increased the level of activities of civil associations. The launch of Structural Adjustment Programmes (SAP) in 1986 increased economic hardship. These developments further deepened the grievances of the wider population (Ikelegbe 2001b). The period between 1988 and 1990 saw widespread public protests against SAPs. The protests were met with a range of government strategies, including 'political manipulation, populist side-payments, elite dispensations, expansion of the parallel economy and overt repression' (Lewis 1996: 88). Civil society responded with further demonstrations and strikes. But the focus of the protests between 1990 and 1993 had shifted from opposing SAPs to protesting against human rights abuses and government policies, and demanding democratization (Ikelegbe 2001b).[2]

When Babangida took power in 1985, he promised to return the country to civilian rule in 1990, which was later postponed to 1993. The military junta kept the move towards democracy closely controlled. In October 1989, in preparation for the elections, the military government established two political parties: the National Republican Convention (NRC), which was 'a little to the right', and the Social Democratic Party (SDP), which was supposed to be 'a little to the left'. Other political parties were prohibited, and the political class and social activists were intimidated (Ihonvbere 1996): 'Tight control of the elections, death threats against dissidents, and press closures . . . reinforced the transition to elected civilian rule, ignoring public opposition to the flawed electoral system' (Adams 1993: 26). The presidential elections did not reinvigorate civil society because the military disabled civil society institutions and completely dominated the political space in the run-up to the elections.

The presidential elections on 12 June 1993 were seen as Nigeria's fairest. The candidate for the SDP, the Yoruba businessman Abiola, emerged as winner. But just two weeks later the military regime annulled the election results. This move had a significant impact on the government–opposition relationship. It reinvigorated 'a dormant society [and] encouraged the formation of scores of pro-democracy and civil liberty organisations' (Ihonvbere 1996: 200). The Campaign for Democracy (CD) compiled the election results from various voting centres and declared Abiola the overwhelming winner over Tofa, the candidate for the NRC. The CD mobilized Nigerians through various affiliations for passive protests against the annulment. In the past, most groups of the generally weak civil society were focused on self-help and providing basic needs for their communities. They lacked a national focus and did not have a political agenda.

Protest and repression under Abacha, 1993–9

The annulment of the 1993 presidential elections united a variety of civil society groups in protest, including the National Association of Democratic

Lawyers, the National Association of Nigerian Students, the Nigerian Union of Journalists, and Women in Nigeria (Ihonvbere 1996). These groups could capitalize on widespread discontent among the population, and thus organize demonstrations and strikes against the annulment. The activities of the CD in particular had a profound impact on civil society in Nigeria (Ihonvbere and Vaughan 1995). During a World Cup qualifying match, the CD distributed leaflets, calling for 'one week of national protest to force Babangida to go and to enforce the result of the June 12 election' (CD leaflet, quoted in Ihonvbere 1996: 202). The CD stressed that the protest was for democracy and not for Abiola as an individual. The leaflet also asked for non-violent and united action, across ethnic religious, geographical and political divisions (Ihonvbere 1996). Between 5 and 9 July 1993, five days of non-violent protest were a success: 'For the first time in Nigeria's post-civil war history the military dictators were openly challenged by millions who took a stand for religious, class, and gender lines' (Ihonvbere 1996: 202).

The military junta reacted with a mix of repression and co-optation. It arrested and assassinated leaders of the pro-democracy movement to instil fear in the population. It closed universities and newspapers. At the same time, it co-opted and bribed factions of the two political parties and members of the national assembly (Aiyede 2003; Ihonvbere 1996). The military regime negotiated with members of the NRC and with the faction of the SDP that had supported Abiola's opponent for the SDP nomination, to set up an Interim National Government (ING). On 26 August 1993, General Babangida resigned, and the ING was announced, led by Chief Ernest Shonekan, with General Sani Abacha as Defence Minister. But, in the face of continuing protests, strikes and economic decline, the military became restless once again. On 17 November 1993, a military coup by Abacha ended Shonekan's regime. This coup was supported by some leaders of the pro-democracy movement, as Abacha, like his predecessors, managed to co-opt them into collaboration. This move was completely rejected by grassroots pro-democratic forces (Ihonvbere 1996). While, in Chile, particularly for the left-wing groups, opposition leaders were more extreme than the masses, the opposite was the case in Nigeria. The civilian political class behaved opportunistically and was often compliant with the military regime. This behaviour instilled in the general population a distrust of political leaders (Lewis 1999).

Abacha created a national conference to prepare for political transition. The conference consisted mainly of conservatives, who were rewarded for their loyalty and support with profitable positions. At the same time, he waged a 'virtual war' (Ihonvbere 1996: 206) against the Nigerian Labour Congress, human rights groups, pro-democracy movements and students. Further confrontations developed between the military junta and the pro-democracy movement, as the first anniversary of the 12 June 1993 elections approached. In May 1994, the National Democratic Coalition (NADECO), a multi-ethnic pro-democracy pressure group, was formed by eminent

Nigerian politicians, retired military officers, human rights activists and business executives. Supported by NADECO, Abiola declared himself the legitimate president, one year after the annulled elections. He was arrested by the military junta and charged with treason. This act sparked the strongest opposition to Abacha yet. Petroleum workers' unions went on strike on 9 July and successfully paralysed the country for nine weeks. They were 'soon joined by disgruntled bank employees and prodemocracy academics, as scattered protests and rioting erupted in several southwestern cities' (Lewis 1999: 147). With a harsh response, Abacha eventually ended the strikes in early September. Activists and leaders of the pro-democracy movement were arrested, harassed and murdered, the media were shut down, while over 120 street protesters were killed (Ihonvbere 1996; Lewis 1999). Additionally, Abacha was able to utilize the opportunism of the political elites and co-opted former chairmen of the SDP and NRC into his government. He consolidated his rule, using a variety of strategies:

> divide civil society by playing groups against each other; bribe, misinform and co-opt; intimidate the leaders of protests and their organisations into silence; contain restless communities, especially the minorities, across the country; rehabilitate discredited politicians and retired military leaders; continue the system of graft, waste, and mismanagement; consolidate the power of the armed forces; and postpone the transition to civil rule for as long as possible.
>
> (Ihonvbere 1996: 206)

Opposition groups were unable to mobilize large-scale dissent since they did not have close links with people across regional, ethnic and religious boundaries. Aiyede (2003) identifies two main groups within civil society. First, there were pro-democracy civic associations, which 'emerged in opposition to the increasing authoritarianism and arbitrariness of the military junta and a growing dissatisfaction among the elites' (Aiyede 2003: 15). These associations included the CD, NADECO and several human rights NGOs, which focused on helping victims of state abuse. Their primary focus was to challenge the annulment of the 1993 presidential elections and to mobilize against military rule. Their members were mainly urban-based elites from Lagos (Lewis 1999). This domination by the urban middle class from the south-west of the country turned the pro-democracy movement into one seen as having a largely southern agenda. The government capitalized on these ethnic, regional and urban versus rural divisions, which further inhibited the creation of a strong and broad-based social movement: 'The pro-democracy movement has not been able to command a grass-roots following nor has it been able to construct a strong national network for the promotion of liberal democratic values in governance' (Aiyede 2003: 21).

The second group focused more narrowly on improving its economic position and opposition economic reform. This group primarily consisted of student movements and labour unions, which had an ethnically based grassroots following. While the pro-democracy associations generally pursued non-violent tactics of civil disobedience, the second group aimed at making the country ungovernable, using more militant and violent activities (Aiyede 2003). They became particularly visible under democratic rule, once the severe climate of threat and intimidation under Abacha had subsided.

Abacha ruled by decrees that were backdated, and continued to use repression and intimidation to suppress any opposition. To prevent any further mass actions in commemoration of the 12 June 1993 elections, in March 1995 'the military junta initiated an unprecedented crackdown on civil society' (Ihonvbere 1996: 211). As part of this crackdown, Abacha jailed members of the Nigerian elite, including General Olusegun Obasanjo for an alleged coup attempt. A public execution of 40 armed robbers in July 1995 further contributed to the climate of fear and intimidation (Ihonvbere 1996). After the execution of the 'Ogoni Nine', which included the activist and author Ken Saro-Wiwa, in November of the same year, the security and intelligence agencies were allowed to act more leniently. Repression and political assassinations became even more frequent. Abacha had successfully created a climate of fear, and had effectively weakened the political and civil society under his rule. He died on 8 June 1998.

Following the chain of succession, Abacha was succeeded by Chief of Defence Staff, General Abdulsalami Abubakar. Abubakar freed almost all political prisoners, including Obasanjo, and generally improved respect for basic human rights. He also oversaw the transition to civilian rule. On 29 May 1999, Olusegun Obasanjo was inaugurated as civilian president, ending 16 years of consecutive military rule. However, civil society was subdued and eroded due to persistent repression and a devastated economy (Lewis 1999).

The nature of protest and repression under the Fourth Republic

Under the civilian regime of the Fourth Republic, civil society organizations remained weak and unable to successfully influence politics. This facilitated the rise of more violent and militant opposition groups, which gained support and became increasingly active under the democratic regime. Their increased visibility was further aided by high levels of poverty, as these militias were able to recruit unemployed youths (Aiyede 2003). These groups and militias were most often ethnic based, and engaged in violent confrontations both with each other and the state. Organized associations often lost control over their members, which were dominated by youth groups, which tended towards criminality and anarchy, resulting in a state of emergency – one of the signs that democracy has not been able to establish legitimacy and control in Nigeria. In 1999 alone, over 200 violent clashes occurred, involving such militant groups (Ikelegbe 2001b). In November 2000, the Oodua Peoples Congress, a militant Yoruba nationalist organization, initiated violent conflicts, which led the federal government to ban all ethnic militias across the country, while Delta state governments also banned all youth associations (Aiyede 2003).

Ikelegbe (2001b) argues that, under the Fourth Republic, attention moved from demilitarization and democratization to more primordial interests. At the same time, the repression, corruption and manipulation that characterized the years of military rule, had diminished the authority of the state. This, combined with widespread poverty and general economic decline, increased the frustration of the masses and facilitated mobilization and radicalization, particularly of youths.

While some parts of society became increasingly violent, the majority of the population withdrew further from the state. Aiyede (2003) argues that distrust of political leaders, combined with repression and economic decline, resulted in political disengagement. This disengagement took the form of a rise in the informal economy and an increase in grassroots groups that focused on self-help and survival: 'The massive growth of grassroots associational life is more an expression of disdain, disengagement, and retreat from the state than new forms of civic engagement with it' (Aiyede 2003: 20). The relationship between the government and non-government actors under the Fourth Republic are therefore characterized by two divergent dynamics. While this relationship is, for the most part, characterized by disengagement and distrust, the government is battling communal, ethnic and religious violence between disenfranchised and militant groups in society.

Oil and the conflict in the Niger Delta

One major focal point of the government–protest nexus in Nigeria is the Niger Delta. The oil resources of the Niger Delta have provided Nigeria's most important export earnings. While the north of the country benefited from the petroleum industry, the ethnic minorities living in the Niger Delta have repeatedly complained about the exploitation of their land, and protested for better economic conditions and more political power (Bob 2002). This section explores the dynamics between the opposition in the Niger Delta and the government under military rule, and the democratic regime since 1999. Ikelegbe argues that

> the manner of conduct of the struggle and resistance of the ND [Niger Delta] people represents the greatest challenge to state authority since the Nigerian civil war, as well as the greatest manifestation of state repression in response to civil challenge to its authority.
>
> (Ikelegbe 2001a: 438)

During the 1970s and 1980s, protests by communities in the Niger Delta consisted mainly of uncoordinated events against the state and multinational oil corporations. These activities were led by traditional community leaders, and included writing petitions and blocking the access routes of the oil corporations (Ikelegbe 2001a). The Movement for the Survival of the Ogoni People (MOSOP) became the best-known group because it successfully attracted widespread international attention, although the Ogoni number only about half a million people. Their protest mainly took the form of non-violent dissent. In 1990, MOSOP presented the Ogoni Bill of Rights to the Nigerian federal government and several international organizations. They campaigned 'to popularize the Ogoni's plight and solicit support for their struggle' (Osaghae 1995: 335). Their call for political autonomy was ignored by the government. MOSOP then turned to the oil companies. In December 1992, MOSOP leaders wrote to the three main oil companies operating in Ogoniland, demanding compensation for damages, the payment of royalties and an immediate halt to environmentally damaging practices. In response the oil companies tightened their security and the government banned any mass actions by the Ogonis. Despite severe threats from the state, a mass rally was held on 3 January 1993. There were no clashes between the protesters and the security forces, but Ken Saro-Wiwa and other MOSOP leaders were arrested. The Ogoni continued their non-violent dissent by holding a mass vigil throughout Ogoniland a few months later (Osaghae 1995).

With the annulment of the June 1993 elections, however, the fight of ethnic minorities intensified. The protests that followed the annulment 'further provided a major impetus for the articulation of the region's grievances and consequently orchestrated a flowering of ethnic and pan-ethnic Niger Delta civil society' (Ikelegbe 2001a: 441). The repressive state response by Abacha to these protests was targeted particularly at MOSOP. In May 1994, four Ogoni chiefs were killed. By this time, MOSOP was divided on how best to continue its fight. The murdered chiefs had opposed Ken Saro-Wiwa's leadership; he was arrested for the killing and 'convicted in a patently unfair trial before a special tribunal' (Bob 2002: 396). Saro-Wiwa claimed that the killings had been provoked by the government. On 10 November 1995, Saro-Wiwa was hanged and, until the end of Abacha's rule, the Ogoni were harshly repressed. During this time, MOSOP was active mostly outside the borders of Nigeria.

The Niger Delta hosts a large number of civil society groups, including communal and ethnic groups, youth associations and pan-ethnic groups. Ikelegbe (2001a) argues that youth and communal groups have generally pursued more violent forms of dissent, while ethnic and regional groups have been focused more on dialogue. After Abacha's death, and particularly since the return to civilian rule, violent dissent has spiralled out of control. An example of a violent militia that has been active primarily under civilian rule is the Ijaw Youth Council (IYC). The IYC was formed in the Niger Delta in late 1998 as a youth association of the Ijaw ethnic region (Ikelegbe

2001b). In December 1998, it set an ultimatum to oil companies to vacate Ijawland. In response, the government declared a state of emergency in January 1999 and sent a large military deployment. The IYC lost control of some groups, which turned increasingly violent. In early November 1999, members of the IYC killed 12 policemen in Odi, which triggered a brutal reaction by the state (Ikelegbe 2001b). IYC activities were seen as a rebellion that threatened law and order and needed to be crushed at all costs. This response of the government to the IYC was representative of its reaction to violent dissent. The regime has been acting in a very heavy-handed manner, aiming for suppression instead of conflict resolution. Under the democratic regime of Obasanjo, state coercion manifested itself in the form of curfews, states of emergency, troop deployment and violent repression (Ikelegbe 2001a). Civil society continues to challenge the authority and legitimacy of the state. The Niger Delta has become a 'region of insurrection, because of the scale of protests, frequency of occupation and disruption of oil production and violent confrontations with the state' (Ikelegbe 2001a: 463).

Summarizing the dynamics

One of the main features of the relationship between the state and the opposition in Nigeria is the weakness and ineffectiveness of the 'political' civil society. By 'political' civil society, I mean groups that aim to influence government and politics, as opposed to self-help grassroots organizations. This ineffectiveness can be attributed to a variety of reinforcing factors. Poor economic performance and the prevalence of neopatrimonialism meant that opposition leaders could be co-opted into government. In particular, the military regime had substantial leverage over opposition leaders, who could either join the dominant state apparatus and gain access, via corruption and neopatrimonialism, to otherwise unattainable resources (Agbaje 1990; Ihonvbere 1996), or face arrest and harassment. This opportunism of political opposition leaders created mistrust among activists and the general population. The result was that civil society was not divided along vertical lines between different groups representing different political interests, each encompassing a grassroots basis and a leadership. Instead, it was characterized by horizontal divisions, where elites and leadership were disengaged and disconnected from activists and the general population. Under these conditions, a sustained and powerful social movement could not be mobilized. Additionally, the pro-democracy movement was largely an urban middle-class phenomenon, unable to engage broader society (Ikelegbe 2001b). As a result of severe poverty, civil society groups lack autonomy and are therefore dependent on foreign donors, and sometimes the state. Competing for donor funds encourages opportunism and can lead to conflicts between interest groups. These conflicts are further aggravated by divisions along ethnic, regional and sectional lines (Ikelegbe 2001b).

Civil society continued to carry out organized protests and demonstrations. In the late 1980s, its focus was on protesting against the implementation of SAP and economic deprivation. In the early 1990s, its attention was primarily directed against human rights abuses and government policies under Babangida. After 1993, demonstrations and strikes were mobilized against the annulment of the presidential elections of that year, and since 1999 most activities have been carried out by youth militias, involved in communal conflicts as well as in the struggle for more rights, economic benefits and environmental protection in the Niger Delta. But dissent in Nigeria has generally been unable to mobilize sustained and broad-based opposition and has, by and large, failed to achieve its objectives.

Part of the reason for this outcome is that civil society was intimidated and effectively constrained under the repressive strategies of the military. The military juntas under Buhari, Babangida and Abacha were very intolerant of dissent and reacted with violent repression to protest, especially to dissent that seemed to be particularly threatening to the make-up of the regime. For example, Babangida, and later Abacha, violently suppressed any pro-democracy movements in the years following the annulment of the June 1993 elections. Another example is the violent response to MOSOP and similar groups demanding political autonomy and access to the most important economic resources of the country. This intolerance towards dissent continues under democratic rule:

> The tendency of the post-colonial state to dominate, subordinate, incorporate and suppress because of its hegemonical, personalistic, patrimonial, authoritarian and absolutist characteristics, and its prevalent abuse, lawlessness, predatoriness, ineptitude and corruption makes the state intolerant to autonomous, civil and popular action.
>
> (Ikelegbe 2001a: 440)

For decades, the military has been the most important and most powerful player (Ihonvbere 1996). The long and influential history of military rule has shaped politics, its institutions, and the perceptions and behaviours of civil society. Political institutions are weak, lack legitimacy and suffer from personalization of power and corruption. Therefore, they are unable to moderate conflicts and facilitate inclusion, participation, negotiation and compromise. With this background, democratic norms and institutions struggle to become entrenched in the political system and wider society. Even after the return to civilian rule in 1999, the Nigerian government continues to use coercion and states of emergency as a tool to deal with discontent.

Apart from its undemocratic past, an additional problem for the Fourth Republic is that dissent has become more violent, partly because the level of fear and intimidation by the state has declined. Ikelegbe argues that civil society groups are using violence as a last resort since peaceful forms of dissent have been unsuccessful. Therefore, 'to secure audience, negotiations, results and adherence to agreements have led the groups towards a violent path' (Ikelegbe 2001a: 459). Civil society groups have adapted their strategies, often over a period of years. For example, MOSOP's initial activities in the early 1990s was primarily peaceful, but as neither the government nor the multinational oil corporations moved to effectively accommodate MOSOP's demands, a more militant and violent group developed within the organization.

CONCLUSION

This chapter has presented the dynamics of the relationship between government and non-government actors in two illustrative case studies. It adopted a micro-level approach to investigating how government and civil society in Chile and Nigeria interact with each other, to show how the protest–repression nexus can play out in particular cases. These case studies demonstrate how the arguments laid out in earlier chapters take shape under specific socio-economic, political and historical circumstances. Both case studies provide further support for the argument that dissent leads to repression and that governments respond more harshly to more threatening and violent dissent. For example, in Chile between 1983 and 1985, severe repression was used to intimidate and end particularly widespread protests and illegal land seizures by shantytown dwellers. In Nigeria, the petroleum workers' strikes, which affected the most important economic activity in the country, as well as violent militia activities in the Niger Delta demanding political autonomy, faced severe repression.

The case studies also highlight the problem that partial democratization poses for the relationship between protest and repression. Since its return to civilian rule in 1999, Nigeria has been classified as a semi-democracy by Polity IV. The government has continued to violate basic human rights and repress dissent. Chile, however, has been classified as a full democracy by Polity IV since its return to a democratic system in 1989; at the same time, the country's human rights record has continuously improved. The evidence from these two cases lends support to the threshold argument (Davenport and Armstrong 2004) that only once democracy has become solidly entrenched in a country will the pacifying effect of democratic norms and institutions be felt. The evidence from Nigeria also lends some support to the proposition of an inverted U-shaped relationship between degree of democracy and repression (Fein 1995), since the level of violence experienced since 1999 exceeds the levels observed during most of Buhari's and Babangida's military rule.

The different levels of repression under different military regimes, as observed in Nigeria and Chile, highlight an interesting aspect of the use of coercion by new governments. The case studies stress that in order to understand, and predict, the extent of repression used by newly installed regimes it is important to take into account the circumstances under which the regimes came into power. After the military coup in Chile in 1973, the new regime immediately behaved particularly violently towards perceived threats from the opposition. The reason for this is twofold. First, by using widespread and severe coercion and repression immediately at the beginning of the regime, the military junta tried to eliminate all opponents and install such levels of fear in the opposition and the wider population that the risk of protest and dissent would be minimal. This strategy was largely successful. Second, the coup, and the new regime, were, at least initially, welcomed by parts of the population. Because during the 'honeymoon period' of Pinochet's rule, repression was primarily directed at left-wing groups, the poor and the working class, he tried not to alienate the middle classes that were originally behind him. In contrast, when Babangida overthrew Buhari in a bloodless counter-coup in 1985, he initially reversed the repressive policies and decisions taken by his predecessors because he partly justified his coup as a necessary means to end the violence of the Buhari regime, which had affected most sections of society and was not based on a left/right division of civil society, as was the case in Chile.

The case studies provide an interesting narrative to the argument that repression leads to dissent. While, in both countries, repression has often led to further or higher levels of protest, the evidence also lends support to the argument for deterrence, meaning that particularly severe and indiscriminately applied repression deters further social mobilization and open forms of opposition. During the first decade of Pinochet's rule, which was particularly violent, dissent took place in only isolated and limited activities. The military regimes in Nigeria were also largely successful in intimidating opposition groups with their iron fist.

Finally, this chapter has highlighted how differences in political experiences and socio-economic conditions affect the prospects for establishing a strong opposition to a repressive and authoritarian government. Chile's long democratic tradition, including its strong political parties, which had a solid and generally broad base in civil society, provided a fertile ground for the mobilization of dissent against Pinochet. Nigeria, however, barely had any democratic history at all. This had a detrimental effect on the nature and strength of dissent: 'The dissolution of the political parties depleted an important organizational base for resistance to the military, and selective government repression against labor, students, academics, human rights groups, and the media proved sufficient to quell large-scale dissent' (Lewis 1999: 146). While, in Chile, political groups were closely linked to society, in Nigeria, the urban middle classes, which formed the core of the opposition, were largely disconnected from wider society. These different conditions and experiences in the two case studies support the arguments for resource mobilization. Resource mobilization theory predicts that countries with dense social networks, like Chile, are more likely to develop a social movement than countries with non-existent, or only loose, social networks, as in

Nigeria (McAdam *et al.* 2001). Additionally, regional, ethnic and religious differences further divided society in Nigeria, acting as a stumbling block to the creation of a sustained and nationwide social movement. Finally, while economic downturns generally destabilized political regimes in Chile, the extreme poverty in Nigeria, combined with its corrupt, hegemonical and neopatrimonial regime, meant that opposition leaders could be co-opted into cooperation, while rural areas in particular became further disengaged and disconnected from the state.

Notes

1 It lasted from 1966 until 1999, with a brief period of the Second Republic between 1979 and 1983.
2 This change in the focus of the protests observed in Nigeria followed a common pattern in Africa, where protest often started in response and opposition to economic policies and poverty, and then mutated into protest against the political regime, demanding political reform (Bratton and van de Walle 1992).

7 Conclusion

This book analyses the dynamics between protest and repression in sub-Saharan Africa and Latin America since the end of the 1970s. The main questions addressed are: How do governments respond to popular protest? Does government repression increase the risk of protest and rebellion? How does the interaction between the government and the opposition differ between democracies, semi-democracies and autocracies? Are there regional-specific characteristics of the interactions between protest, repression and political regimes? I investigated these questions at three different levels of analysis, employing different quantitative analyses and qualitative case studies.

By using a multi-method approach to investigate the link between protest and repression, this book addresses several shortcomings of the literature in this area. The multitude of often contradictory findings has been attributed to a range of factors: heavy reliance on one particular data source, inappropriate measures, ignoring the longitudinal aspect of the interactions and inadequacy of datasets to allow for adequate modelling of complex relationships (Johnston and Mueller 2001). In the introduction to an edited book on repression and mobilization, Davenport (2005) notes that some progress has been made in addressing these shortcomings, but he also highlights aspects that are likely to affect the reliability of our empirical analyses. He argues that, to increase confidence in our findings, it is necessary to test the same models under different settings, using different methodological approaches and different data sources.

I investigated the relationship between protest, repression and political regimes using three sets of analyses. The macro-level study of yearly data from 66 countries from Latin America and sub-Saharan Africa provided a general investigation of how protest affects repression, how repression impacts upon protest, and how the nature of the political regime influences both repression and protest. This analysis distinguished between three types of dissent: peaceful dissent in the form of demonstrations and strikes, small-scale violent dissent in the form of riots, and large-scale violent dissent in the form of guerrilla warfare and rebellion. Repression was captured as varying degrees of life integrity violations, which included political imprisonment, torture, murder and disappearances. Like the majority of the literature in this field, the macro-level analyses investigated the two causal directions – one leading from protest to repression, the other from repression to protest – independently of one another.

The second set of analyses made the two-way dynamics between protest and repression the core of the investigation. Vector autoregression models, which are specifically designed to test interrelationships between variables, were used to analyse the two-way relationship between protest and repression. For this analysis, I used daily data from six Latin American and three African countries, to capture the reciprocity between the government and the opposition's behaviour. To explore the influence of regime type on the dynamics between protest and repression, I disaggregated the nine countries into democratic, semi-democratic and authoritarian sub-sets, ending up with 18 separate time-series analyses. Whereas the macro-level analysis concentrated on physical acts of dissent and the violation of life integrity rights, the time-series analyses broadened the understanding of the concepts of protest and repression. For the VAR analyses of the individual countries, those behaviours were conceptualized on a wider continuum, ranging from verbal statement to violent acts. Additionally, accommodating behaviour was incorporated in the analysis of domestic conflict to investigate how the accommodating behaviour of one actor influences the behaviour of the other actor.

Finally, the third empirical investigation was located at the micro level, presenting two case studies of Nigeria and Chile. Tracking the interactions between the government and the opposition in Chile under General Pinochet until the early years of the Alfonsín administration, and in Nigeria under military rule from 1983–99 and the following presidency of Obasanjo, I showed how the theoretical arguments and the results of quantitative analyses presented in the preceding chapters, played out under specific circumstances.

The three sets of empirical investigation largely supported the theoretical arguments put forward in Chapter 2. The macro-level analysis showed that repression leads to protest and that protest leads to repression. It also supported the argument that more violent threats to the government's authority trigger a more violent response from the state's security apparatus. Riots, guerrilla warfare and rebellions substantially increase the risk of repression, while the effect of peaceful demonstrations and strikes seems to be negligible. These results were also confirmed using daily data and a different statistical methodology. The time-series analyses in Chapter 5 showed that, in most cases, protest led to repression. Finally, the case studies of Nigeria and Chile provided further support for this argument that protesting against one's own government is a dangerous undertaking, particularly under military rule. Pinochet, Buhari, Babangida and Abacha confronted strikes and demonstrations against their leadership with an iron fist.

Turning the direction of causality around, the results from the macro-level analysis suggest that repression does not work as a deterrent against dissent.

When governments violate the basic rights of their citizens, by arresting them for political reasons, torturing and even killing them, they are likely to be faced with resistance. The findings also indicate that the more severe repression is, the more severe the form of dissent becomes as well. Hence, governments would be ill advised to assume that they can minimize potential threats by torturing and killing their opponents. But, as the case studies highlight, using severe repression can sometimes be effective in sufficiently intimidating the population and in weakening the organized opposition to stall dissent – at least for a limited time period. This outcome is especially likely when the general population is completely disengaged from politics and the state, and the opposition leadership is easily co-opted by the government and lacks close links to grassroots organizations.

The analyses also provide consistent support for the argument that protest and repression, once initiated, are likely to continue. Both Nigeria and Chile provide examples of recurrent protests. Once opposition groups – for example, labour unions, political parties or pro-democracy organizations – manage to organize a successful strike or demonstration against the regime, this often sets the stage for a series of consecutive protest activities. These series of dissent can unfold either over a few days, like the five days of widespread protest in Nigeria during July 1993, or months, as in Chile, where the opposition staged protests almost every month between 1983 and 1986, or even as yearly events on politically significant anniversaries. An example of such an 'anniversary protest' is the protests and demonstrations against the annulment of the June 1993 elections in Nigeria.

The results of the macro-level analysis in Chapter 3 also show that protest activities tend to continue from one year to the next. Distinguishing between different types of protest, the results highlight that less threatening protest activities often function as a precursor and build-up of more severe forms of dissent. In fact, the most likely effect of peaceful protest is not that it continues with the same intensity, but that it escalates into large-scale violent dissent. These dynamics are further highlighted by several examples from the case studies. In Chile during the mid-1980s, left-wing opposition groups, in particular the FPMR (Frente Patriótico Manuel Rodríguez), adopted more and more violent tactics, which eventually contributed to the split, and substantial weakening, of the opposition. In Nigeria, similar trends could be observed. By the mid-1990s, the leadership of MOSOP (the Movement for the Survival of the Ogoni People) disagreed on tactics of dissent, where some wanted to depart from their main strategies of non-violence. Another example are civil society groups in the Niger Delta, where particularly since the end of the Abacha regime in 1999, the violence committed by youth groups had spiralled out of control.

The side of the government is similarly affected by these self-perpetuating tendencies towards violence and repression. Governments in Nigeria, both military and civilian, have repeatedly declared states of emergency to tackle protest and dissent. In Chile, various security agencies contributed to the continuation of torture, killings and arbitrary arrests. The macro-level analysis presented in Chapter 3 also shows that once governments make concessions to the respect for life integrity rights, they find themselves on a slippery slope. The level of repression employed by governments tends to get worse over time. And, once severe repression occurs, the risk of this kind of coercion occurring in the following year increases substantially. This highlights how important it is to prevent the outbreak of repression in the first place, including coercion that happens initially only on a limited scale.

One of the main arguments of this book is that the nature of the political regime – meaning the degree of democracy present in the political institutions – plays an important role in understanding and regulating the dynamics between protest and repression. The statistical analysis of the 66 Latin American and African countries provides further support for the hypothesis that democratic political institutions constitute a method of nonviolence (Rummel 1997). Governments in democratic countries are more likely than their counterparts in authoritarian countries to respect the life integrity rights of their citizens. The vector autoregression models also show that in all authoritarian cases past repression led to further repression, while this was the case in only four out of six democratic cases. The results of the macro-level analysis, however, also reveal that the pacifying effect of democracy only kicks in for those countries that have fully democratized, although this positive effect is noticeable earlier, meaning in less fully democratized countries, in Africa than it is in Latin America. This finding supports the threshold model put forward by Davenport and Armstrong (2004), who argue that only for the most democratic countries is there a negative linear relationship between democracy and repression. The macro-level analysis of repression also shows that democratic institutions dampen a government's reaction to dissent. Although in democracies the risk of coercion still increases when protest occurs, it does so to a substantially lower level than in countries that do not qualify as democracies. The results from the VAR models also suggest that democracy is no guarantee that governments would not attempt to limit dissent using conflictual behaviour. Even democratic governments are unlikely to simply tolerate the display of opposition and protest.

The case studies highlight interesting differences between how fully established democracies and semi-democracies deal with dissent. After the democratic elections in Chile in December 1989, open protest – for example, in the form of illegal land seizures – was frowned upon by the government, as well as by most sections of society. Leaders of civil society and social movements themselves encouraged the use of official, institutionalized channels to get their grievances heard, therefore reducing the level and intensity of dissent. The democratic government also made it clear that such dissent would undermine the democratic system and could therefore not be tolerated. But this rejection of protest did not result in the use of violence or repression by the state. In Nigeria, with the beginning of the Fourth Republic under President

Obasanjo in 1999, the display of dissent did not decline; instead militias, and in particular youth associations, became more violent. The government responded with curfews, states of emergency and repression. Due to the long history of military rule, pervasive neopatrimonialism and personalization of political power, the civilian regime lacks the legitimacy and institutions to channel, and respond to, dissent in a cooperative and constructive fashion.

In Chapter 2, I argued that the display of dissent and protest should be less common in democracies. In such regimes, the opposition is expected to have available to it, and make use of, institutionalized channels to voice its discontent and to have its grievances heard. As mentioned above, this was indeed the case in Chile. With the end of Pinochet's rule, the social movement also came to a halt. Both government and opposition, as well as society at large, favoured the use of institutionalized channels over dissent and protest for influencing and participating in politics. The macro-level analysis, however, could not confirm any strong relationship between degree of democracy and the probability of protest. But the results of the time-series analyses of the individual countries show that in democracies, repression is more likely to lead to protest than in semi-democracies or autocracies. In five out of six analyses of democracies, protest followed repression, whereas this was the case in only five out of eight semi-democracies and in only two out of four autocracies. These results support the argument that in a fully institutionalized democracy, people expect their government to respect the freedoms of their citizens – and are willing to protest if the state steps over the line and infringes the rights of its people. At the same time, these models also suggest that, in autocracies, the opposition does not pursue a hard line against the government in the face of repression due to fear of serious repercussions. However, in a democracy, the opposition appears to be more confident in not giving in to the regime, even in the face of hostile government actions. It can be speculated that, in democracies, the opposition is more confident that negative state sanctions will not escalate so that the benefits of not cooperating with a hostile government outweigh the costs of pursuing a hard line.

Finally, this book has investigated whether, and how, the relationship between protest, repression and political regimes played out differently in Latin America compared to sub-Saharan Africa. The macro-level analysis shows that the general trends of the interactions were very similar between the two regions, but it also hints at some differences. Between 1977 and 2002, governments in Latin American were more repressive than their African counterparts. This observation was independent of regime type: Latin American authoritarian rulers were more repressive than African authoritarian rulers, while democratic governments in Latin America were more repressive than democratic governments in Africa. The results also show that the pacifying effect of democracy on government behaviour kicked in earlier – meaning for countries that were not as democratic – in Africa than in Latin America. When faced with dissent, governments in Latin America reacted more harshly than their African counterparts. The extent and severity of repression was more limited in Africa than in Latin America, even in the face of internal threats and opposition. One of the explanations for this particularly repressive behaviour of Latin American governments could be that, in these countries, the repressive apparatus was generally more institutionalized, better equipped, often larger and more effective than in Africa. As a result, governments in Latin America were far better 'equipped' to use widespread repression against their perceived, or real, enemies, leading to higher levels of repression in Latin American than in Africa.

Another contributing factor for the more repressive behaviour of Latin American compared to African governments is that the opposition was more active and more organized in Latin America. As highlighted in the case studies, civil society and opposition groups were far stronger in Latin America compared to Africa. Opposition and social movement groups can, in most cases, build on a long history and tradition in Latin America. In Chile, opposition parties were well developed, so that the period of military rule was unable to destroy them or render them ineffective. Instead, they were able to activate their followers, together with trades unions and various other organizations, and mobilize widespread and resilient opposition against the regime. In Africa, on the other hand, society was split not along vertical lines, dividing different groups with different interests and relationships to government, but along horizontal lines, separating political leaders, both from the opposition and pro-government groups, from grassroots groups and the population at large. Due to the nature of the political and economic system in Africa, leaders of opposition groups could generally be co-opted into collaboration with government, therefore withdrawing support, leadership and independence from opposition groups. As a result, grassroots groups were often more radical than opposition leadership, whereas the opposite was often the case in Latin America. Leaders of social movements pursued violent tactics, which were rejected by their general following. These dynamics are also reflected in the case studies of Chile and Nigeria, in Chapter 6. In Chile, the violence pursued by radical Communist groups contributed to the split in the opposition, while, in Nigeria, the government was generally successful in co-opting members of the opposition into cooperation, leaving dissident groups to be dominated by disenfranchised and disillusioned violent youths.

Another factor that contributed to the weakness of civil society in Africa was that opposition activists generally came from a particular background, which left those groups disconnected from the general population, and therefore unable to mobilize broad-based and sustained social movements and resistance to the regime. In Nigeria, whose experience is representative of that of other African countries, the protest movement for the return to democracy was overwhelmingly dominated by the urban middle classes, by professionals and students (Bratton and van de Walle 1992; Ihonvbere 1996; Wiseman 1986). These groups were unable to mobilize the generally disengaged wider society. Additionally, rulers in Nigeria, and other African countries, have successfully employed the strategy of 'divide and rule'. They have been able to further divide and weaken their opposition by provoking primordial sentiments in order to incite ethnic, religious and communal differences and conflicts.

POLICY IMPLICATIONS AND DIRECTIONS FOR FUTURE RESEARCH

So what are the main practical or policy-relevant conclusions that can be drawn from the insights gained from these investigations? The findings from the multi-method analysis of the relationship between protest, repression and political regimes suggest several recommendations. The results from the three different sets of analyses have highlighted again the importance of conflict prevention at the earliest stages. They emphasize the importance of regulating discontent and conflict between government and opposition as soon as these divisions become noticeable. To prevent conflict and violence, it is crucial to channel disagreements as soon as they manifest themselves, using institutional channels, in order to deal with them in a regulated, safe and transparent manner. It is important to work towards positive engagement of the opposing factions and to encourage accommodating and cooperative behaviour, before one of the parties starts off on the slippery slope to confrontation. While in recent years more research has focused on identifying potentially conflictual situations and countries at risk of repression (e.g. Carment 2003; Harff 2003; Poe *et al.* 2006), more work on early warning and risk assessment is needed to provide the policy community with more timely and useable information to prevent the outbreak of conflict and violence.

The results of the various analyses further emphasize the importance of well-established and strong democratic political institutions. Democracy can be an effective tool in minimizing conflict and internal violence, but merely holding elections is not sufficient to achieve this goal. Instead, political institutions need to be seen as legitimate, and outside the manipulation and control of individual leaders, in order to be effective and utilized for resolving disagreements and conflicts.

For a democratic political system to be effective, different groups within and outside the political system, such as opposition parties, the media, professional associations, as well as groups based in rural areas, need to be strengthened. Even within a democratic set-up, such groups need to be able to operate independently of government influence and control in order to foster a vibrant civil society and to create a viable counterweight to the power of the state. As the Nigerian example highlights, for civil society groups to contribute to peaceful conflict resolution and collaboration with government, it is important that those groups are internally ruled and run according to democratic norms (e.g. Brysk 2000; Ikelegbe 2001b).

The Nigerian case study further emphasizes the need for, and importance of, economic development. Under conditions of severe poverty, where virtually all avenues to influence, power and economic well-being are via the state, it is almost impossible to build a strong and independent civil society and effective political opposition. Economic development is necessary in order to reduce the dominating position of state. At the same time, however, economic development is certainly no guarantee that conflict between the government and the opposition can be avoided. As the macro-level analyses show, the economically better-off Latin American countries were at the same time also more repressive than the poorer African countries. It is important to highlight that the strength of a state can also be used to the detriment of its people. Governments in richer countries are likely to be in a better position to build a strong security apparatus, which could be used against political opponents. The difference in the size and strengths of the repressive agencies in Latin America compared to those in Africa, particularly during the 1980s, has most likely been one of the reasons why Latin American governments have used more violence and coercion than their African colleagues. In fact, research has shown that it is important to control and constrain the powers of the executive in order to avoid the misuse of a country's security apparatus (Colaresi and Carey 2008).

Finally, we need to develop a better understanding of the conditions for cooperation and peaceful conflict resolution. Most of our theories and empirical models are geared towards understanding conflict, not cooperation and peace. We need more systematic research into the conditions of peace in order to better understand why we observe peace and cooperation in situations where we would expect repression and violence. A better understanding of the conditions and dynamics that facilitate and enable peaceful resolutions is needed to avoid the use and escalation of violence between governments and their citizens.

Appendix: Socio-economic background of countries in the IPI dataset

Economic wealth not only influences the strength of the state, but also its success and therefore acceptance among the population. It affects the wealth and resources of the population, as well as the opportunity costs for them that are attached to participating in protest activities. The degree of urbanization and the size of the population have an impact on the communication structure among the population and influence the ability to mobilize protest and dissent.

All nine countries from the IPI data are middle powers, which means that their international importance is relatively similar. Therefore, it can be assumed that differences in the results are not caused by different levels of importance of particular countries in the international system. Looking at the economic background of the nine countries, they are roughly divided into two groups with respect to economic wealth and growth. Table A.1 shows the main summary statistics of GNP per capita in the nine countries.

The three African countries are much poorer than the Latin American countries in terms of GNP per capita. The nine countries are equally

Table A.1 Summary statistics of GNP per capita

	Minimum	Maximum	Mean	Std dev.
Argentina	2610	6110	3448.14	974.61
Brazil	1580	2760	2192.63	446.73
Chile	1410	2860	1987.64	433.90
Colombia	1190	1300	1232.56	36.61
Mexico	1960	3490	2410.00	513.19
Venezuela	2630	4570	3392.00	631.45
Nigeria	310	1180	712.96	343.47
Zaire	170	640	366.11	145.32
Zimbabwe	540	890	688.18	124.25

Source: World Bank World Development Indicators, mean of yearly values of GNP per capita in US$

distributed over three groups, depending on whether they experienced a relatively steady increase, a decrease, or both growth and decline during the observed time period. Argentina, Brazil and Mexico experienced relatively consistent economic growth during the time period of interest. Venezuela, Nigeria and Zaire suffered from a steady decline in GNP per capita. And Chile, Colombia and Zimbabwe make up the last category of countries that underwent various ups and downs in their GNP per capita.

The countries also vary along the indicator of urbanization, where Nigeria is the country with the largest percentage of the population living in urban areas. The nine countries have very different socio-economic structures. In the following, I outline the main developments in the nine countries that occurred during the time period on which the analysis concentrates.

COUNTRY PROFILE: ARGENTINA

Compared to the other countries in the sample, Argentina has relatively low levels of domestic political conflict, both comparing the mean and the maximum values of protest and repression. It is the most ethnically homogeneous country in the sample, as well as the one that encountered the largest increase in GNP per capita over the observed time period. It also has the highest GNP per capita on average. The IPI dataset on Argentina starts on 1 April 1982 and ends on 31 December 1992. Hence, the 'dirty war' during 1975–7 is not covered in the observed time span. The data start just one day prior to Argentina's occupation of the Falkland/Malvinas islands on

Table A.2 Demographic indicators

	Urbanization[a]	*Population[b]*
Argentina	11.45	31245145
Brazil	17.04	142000000
Chile	16.28	12268103
Colombia	30.10	32241296
Mexico	42.26	79979755
Venezuela	20.59	18204550
Nigeria	94.67	84724948
Zaire	15.53	30713820
Zimbabwe	18.26	7086045

a Source: US Bureau of the Census, International Database, urban population as percentage of total population; average of yearly values during observed time period
b Source: World Bank World Development Indicators (WDI); average of yearly values during observed time period

2 April 1982. After the humiliating surrender of the Argentine military to the British in June of the same year, Argentina returned to civilian rule. For most of the time period covered, Argentina was a relatively well-established democracy. On 30 October 1983, Raúl Ricardo Alfonsín, leader of the Radical Party, was elected president. The following years saw economic recession and increasing inflation, which approached almost 700 per cent in 1985. During the same year, the government declared a state of siege for October and November as a response to a series of bomb attacks. The late 1980s were characterized by further inflation and increasing unemployment, as well as strikes by trades unions. During a severe economic crisis in mid-1989, President Alfonsín declared the state of siege as a reaction to looting and rioting in the cities. This created the opportunity for the Peronists to return to government. In the presidential elections on 14 May 1989, Carlos Saúl Menem from the Peronist Party was elected president. Facing increasing economic pressure and food riots, Alfonsín resigned six months prior to the end of his term. Menem granted pardons to previous military leaders who had been imprisoned for human rights violations during the 1970s and 1980s. This attempt to pacify the military, as well as further increases in inflation and unemployment, led to various protests, as well as the declaration of the state of siege during the early 1990s.

COUNTRY PROFILE: BRAZIL

The IPI data on Brazil range from the beginning of April 1983 until the end of December 1992. During that time, Brazil experienced comparatively low-intensity levels of protest and repression. Looking at socio-economic indicators, such as GNP per capita, ethnic fractionalization and urbanization, Brazil falls into the middle category of the nine Latin American and African countries of the dataset. However, Brazil has extremely unequal income distribution and suffers from bad social welfare. It is also the most populous country in the sample. Similar to Argentina, Brazil enters the analysis towards the end of an extended period of military rule, which lasted from 1964 to 1985. In indirect elections in 1985, Tancredo Neves took the presidency from the military President João Figueiredo, who had continued the liberalization process started under his predecessor, Ernesto Geisel. Shortly after Neves was elected, he fell ill and vice-president José Sarney became president. During his presidency, the influence of the military on politics was still very strong. In 1989, Fernando Collor de Mello won the presidential elections and was in power until he resigned after a corruption scandal in September 1992. During April 1983 and December 1992, Brazil experienced military rule for part of the time, indirect elections in 1985 and direct elections in 1989. It had an extraordinarily long and constrained transition from military to civilian rule. Similar to Argentina, it went through high levels of inflation, price increases and economic stability programmes, and encountered several clashes between the police and rioters, workers and students, particularly in the late 1980s.

COUNTRY PROFILE: CHILE

The IPI data on Chile begin in May 1979 and end in October 1992. They cover about ten years of military rule under General Augusto Pinochet and two years of civilian rule under President Patricio Aylwin. Therefore, for most of the time period, Chile ranks very low on the democracy scale. The average value of the Polity variable (Democracy minus Autocracy) is the lowest in all nine countries, with the exception of Zaire. All other countries are, on average, more democratic than Chile. Only Colombia, Nigeria and Zimbabwe experienced similar, or higher, levels of repression on average during the observed time period. With respect to socio-economic aspects, Chile is ethnically relatively homogeneous. Compared to the other countries in the sample, only Argentina has a more ethnically homogeneous population. The level of urbanization is relatively low and very similar to that of Argentina and Brazil. The average GNP per capita of nearly US$2,000 places Chile in the middle category of the nine countries. Inflation rates between 1983 and 1987 were relatively low (20–31 per cent), particularly in comparison to Argentina and Brazil.

Chile had a very strong military regime. After the coup in 1973, Augusto Pinochet established a highly personalized rule. Although the return to a civilian regime was originally scheduled for 1985, a plebiscite in 1980 approved a constitution that kept Pinochet in office until 1990. The hierarchical military, and strong support from important civilian allies, put serious constraints on the transition period (Linz and Stepan 1996: 211). After a referendum in October 1988 against Pinochet's continuation as president until 1997, presidential elections were held on 14 December 1989, which were won by Patricio Aylwin. He took office on 11 March 1990, while Pinochet remained army commander-in-chief.

At the beginning of the Pinochet regime, there was little protest. After the collapse of the economy in 1982, and a sharp rise in unemployment until mid-1983, a strong protest movement developed, which escalated in May to August of the same year. The Pinochet regime was particularly intolerant of labour strikes and popular protest. The average levels of protest and repression decreased substantially after the plebiscite against Pinochet on 5 October 1988 and continued on a downturn after the election of Aylwin on 16 December 1989.

COUNTRY PROFILE: COLOMBIA

After Brazil and Mexico, Colombia is the third most populous country in Latin America. During the 1980s it experienced a substantial increase in urbanization. It is, on average, the third most urbanized country in the sample after Nigeria and Mexico. Although Colombia has a comparatively low GNP per capita, it did not experience the problem of high inflation to the same extent as Argentina, Brazil and Chile.

The IPI data on Colombia range from May 1983 until December 1992. During this time period, Colombia was characterized by high levels of domestic conflict as well as a relatively stable democracy. Only Venezuela has higher democracy scores, on average, during the observed time period. Colombia has a long-standing tradition of a two-party system and a well-developed institutional structure. At the same time, it suffers from the influence of three powerful groups, namely guerrilla groups, drug dealers and death squads: 'The guerrillas desire a new system with more power and benefits for the common people, the drug dealers one in which they can carry out their illicit trade with impunity, and the death squads one without guerrillas or poor people making demands' (Kline 1996).

Between 1983 and 1992, several ceasefires were negotiated, and broken too. One ceasefire in the guerrilla war was achieved under President Belisario Betancur Cuartas in 1984. This was de facto brought to an end with the attack on the Palace of Justice in Bogota on 6/7 November 1985. Members of the guerrilla group M-19 (the Nineteenth of April Movement) took most of the Supreme Court hostage and killed 11 of its members. The attack was then violently suppressed by the army. During the presidency of Virgilio Barco (1986–90), Colombia endured a 'dirty war' between the government, guerrilla groups, drug dealers and paramilitary squads. A peace process got under way in the late 1980s and culminated in a National Assembly writing a new constitution. The new constitution came into effect on 4 July 1991. However, the meeting of the National Assembly in February 1991 was paired with rebel attacks and the bloodiest fighting of the 30-year insurgency.

COUNTRY PROFILE: MEXICO

Mexico is the most urbanized Latin American country in the sample. With respect to ethnic homogeneity it falls in the middle category of the nine countries. During the time period from February 1984 until November 1992, Mexico had, on average, a comparatively large GNP per capita. Despite the drop in oil prices in 1985–6, Mexico did not experience the same level of inflation as Argentina, Brazil or Chile. Between 1984 and 1992, on average, Mexico experienced more intense protest than repression. Under President Miguel de la Madrid (1982–8), the government initiated a shift towards more liberal development strategies. However, the decline of oil prices in 1985–6 led to further weakening of the economy. In 1988, Carlos Salinas de Gortari was elected president, but the elections were marred by allegations of fraud. This led to an increase in domestic political conflict during the following years.

COUNTRY PROFILE: VENEZUELA

Venezuela is the most democratic country, on average, in the sample. It can look back on one of the longest traditions of democracy in Latin America. It also has a relatively homogeneous society, similarly to that of Chile. The data on Venezuela range from March 1983 to December 1992. During that time period, it had the second-largest GNP per capita, which was higher only for Argentina. However, after the world prices for petroleum plunged in early 1983, the economy deteriorated until the late 1980s. Compared to the other eight countries in the sample, the mean values of domestic conflict are relatively low; protest is on average slightly more intense than state coercion. Protest also reaches, in absolute terms, far higher levels of intensity than repression. This is largely due to the urban riots in February 1989. After President Carlos Andrés Pérez (1989–93) took office on 2 February 1989, he announced that the foreign reserves had been exhausted, and declared a restructuring of the political economy (El Gran Viraje – the Great Turnaround). This resulted in the 'worst outbreak of violence since the early 1960s' (Myers 1996: 240).

COUNTRY PROFILE: NIGERIA

Nigeria is the most urbanized country in the sample and the one with the second-largest population behind Brazil. Between January 1983 and December 1992, it had the largest GNP per capita among the three African countries, but still substantially smaller than that of the Latin American countries. Together with Zaire, it has the most ethnically heterogeneous society. This has led to various violent outbreaks between Christians and Muslims, not only during the time covered by dataset but also until the present day. Partly as a result of these conflicts, Nigeria underwent comparatively intense domestic political conflict and, in particular, high levels of state repression, both on average and in absolute terms.

The dataset starts in January 1983, towards the end of the Second Republic (1979–83). In August/September 1983, President Shagari was re-elected for a second term. However, General Mohammed Buhari staged a coup and immediately banned all political parties. A series of military regimes followed. In 1985, General Ibrahim Babangida overthrew Buhari and was in power until 1993, defeating two violent coup attempts during this time. Under his rule, Nigeria experienced a series of violent clashes between

Muslims and Christians, to which he responded with more restrictive rules and regulations and the establishment of a National Guard in May 1992. He also successfully extended the time period of his rule past the initial date of October 1990, which was set for the return to civilian rule. Therefore, apart from the time period of the Second Republic until the end of 1983, Nigeria scored very poor marks on the democracy scale. After Buhari's coup in 1983, the only small move towards a more democratic regime occurred in spring 1989, when Babangida lifted the ban on political activities.

COUNTRY PROFILE: ZAIRE

The IPI data on Zaire span the longest time period compared to the other countries in the sample. They range from January 1975 to December 1992. Since Zaire was not named 'Democratic Republic of Congo' until 1997, I use the country name Zaire throughout this analysis. Mobutu Sese Seko, who took power in 1965, ruled Zaire during the entire time covered by the dataset. Protest and repression spiked during the invasion of Shaba province, formerly known as Katanga, by the Congolese National Liberation Front (FLNC). Two further spikes of protest occurred during the early 1990s, which were caused by widespread and frequent strikes, often violent, calling for democratization and multiparty elections, as well as riots, which were mostly led by students.

Among the nine countries, Zaire is the one with the highest level of ethnic fractionalization. It is also the poorest country in sample, measured by average GNP per capita during the observed time period. On average, it is also the most authoritarian regime. The percentage of the population living in urban areas is comparatively low. Despite the rebels' occupation of territories in the late 1980s, Zaire still has the lowest mean values of conflict intensity, both for dissent and state coercion, although the levels are higher for protest than for repression. The maximum value of protest is substantially larger than that of repression, which is mainly caused by the secession movement and the intense and frequent strikes and protests during the early 1990s.

COUNTRY PROFILE: ZIMBABWE

The data on Zimbabwe start in December 1974 and end in December 1985. They cover the time period of the war for independence and the first five years of independence. The monthly plot of domestic conflict clearly reflects the guerrilla warfare during the fight for independence, particularly at the end of 1976. Most of the friction and fighting occurred between the African National Council (ANC) under Bishop Muzorewa, the Zimbabwe African National Union (ZANU-PF) under Robert Mugabe and the Zimbabwe

African People's Union (ZAPU) under Joshua Nkomo on the one side and the Rhodesian government under Ian Smith on the other. In 1976, ZANU and ZAPU formed a political alliance, the Patriotic Front (PF), building a united front for the fighting and negotiations for independence. After Mugabe was elected in 1980 and initial cooperation between ZANU and ZAPU, the relationship deteriorated and escalated in the mid-1980s when dissident movements in Matabeleland were violently crushed by the Zimbabwean army.

Due to the war of independence in the late 1970s, the maximum values of both protest and repression are comparatively high. Also the mean values of domestic political conflict are relatively high and comparable to those of Chile under the Pinochet regime. Zimbabwe's average GNP per capita during the observed time period was very low and comparable to that of Nigeria. However, its society is substantially more ethnically homogeneous than those of Zaire and Nigeria.

Table A.3 Details of country sets

Name of set	Time period	Polity scores
Argentina I	1 April 1982–30 October 1983	−8
Argentina II	31 October 1983–31 December 1992	8 and 7
Brazil I	1 July 1983–15 January 1985	−3
Brazil II	16 January 1985–31 December 1992	7 and 8
Chile I	7 August 1983–4 October 1988	−6
Chile II	5 October 1988–15 December 1989	−1
Chile III	16 December 1989–30 October 1992	8
Colombia I	1 May 1983–31 December 1992	8 and 9
Mexico I	1 February 1984–13 July 1988	−3
Mexico II	14 July 1988–30 November 1992	0
Venezuela I	1 March 1983–3 February 1992	9 and 8
Nigeria I	1 January 1983–31 December 1983	7
Nigeria II	1 January 1984–3 May 1989	−7
Nigeria III	4 May 1989–31 December 1992	−5
Zaire I	1 January 1975–23 November 1990	−9
Zaire II	24 November 1990–31 December 1992	−8
Zimbabwe I	1 December 1974–30 June 1983[a]	4 and 5
Zimbabwe II	1 July 1983–31 December 1985	1

a One might suggest that it would be more intuitive to divide the time periods for Zimbabwe into two sets before and after independence instead of using the polity scale as a rule for choosing the sets. I used Chow-tests to statistically determine whether there is a significant break in the time series when the then Rhodesia became independent. However, the test was not statistically significant at the 0.5 level.

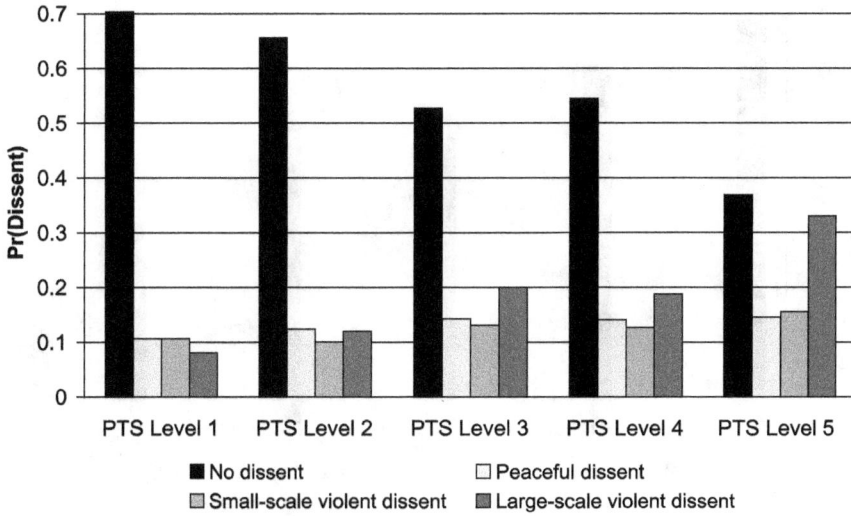

Figure A.1 Dissent as response to repression in autocracies, Latin America.

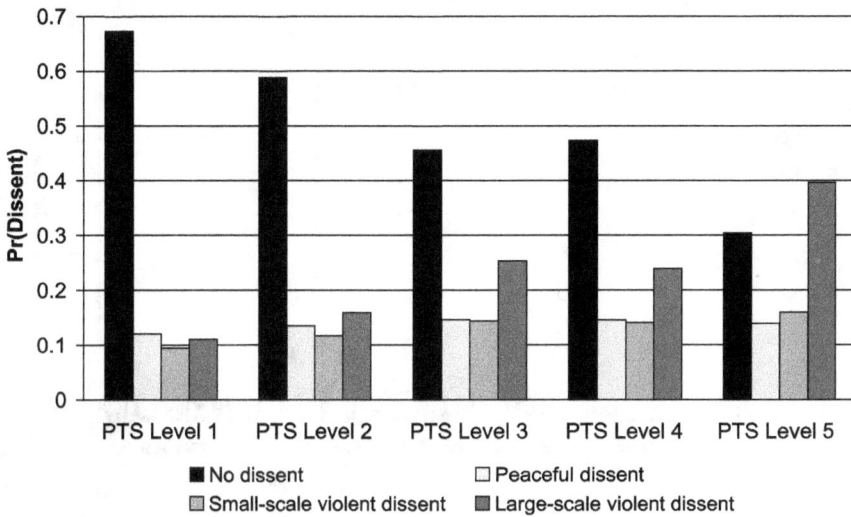

Figure A.2 Dissent as response to repression in semi-democracies, Latin America.

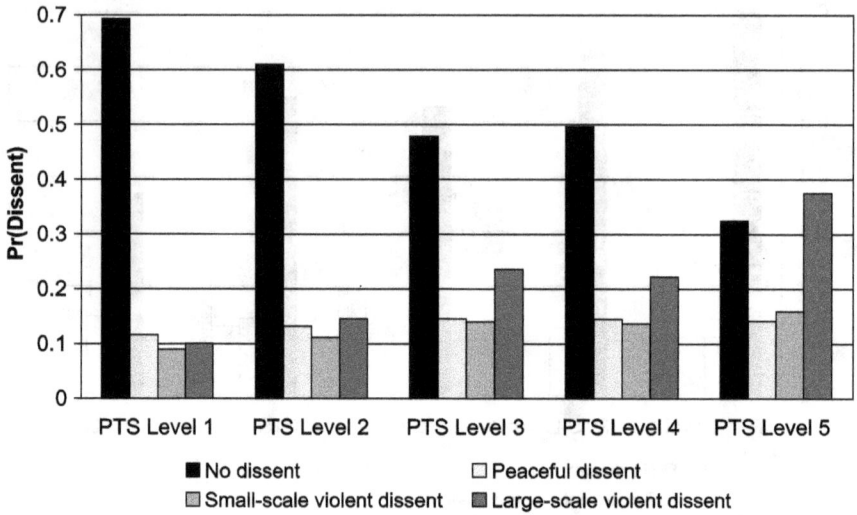

Figure A.3 Dissent as response to repression in democracies, Latin America.

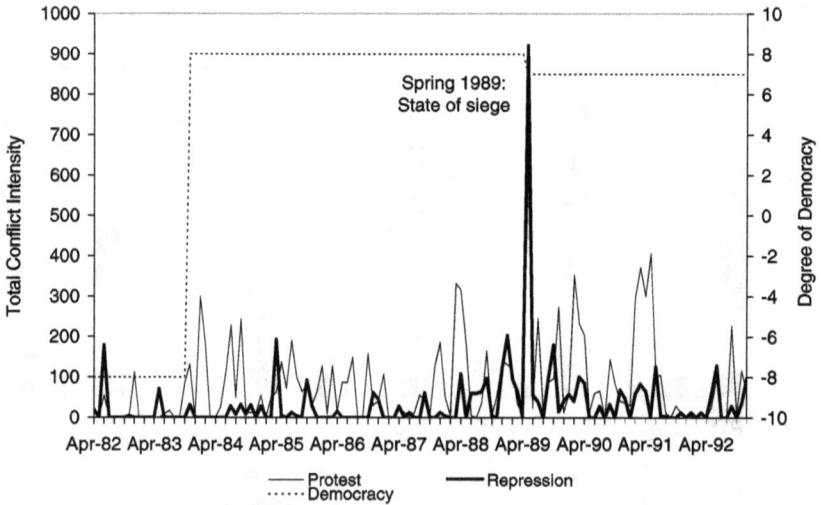

Figure A.4 Argentina, April 1982 to December 1992.

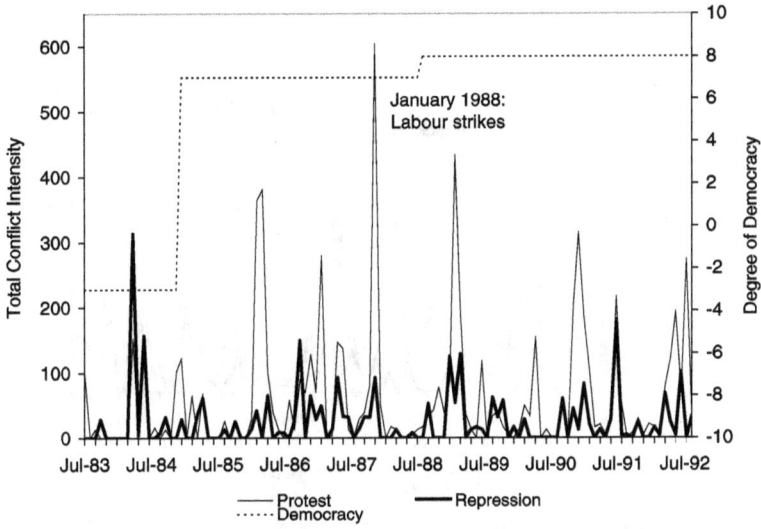

Figure A.5 Brazil, July 1983 to December 1992.

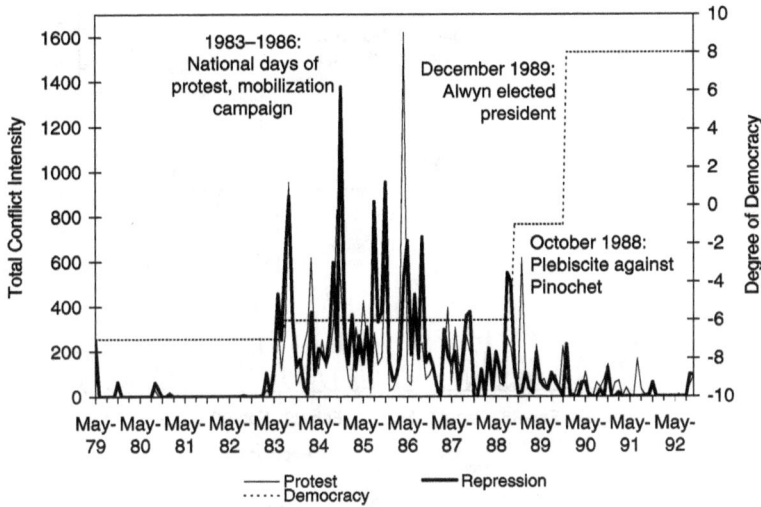

Figure A.6 Chile, May 1979 to October 1992.

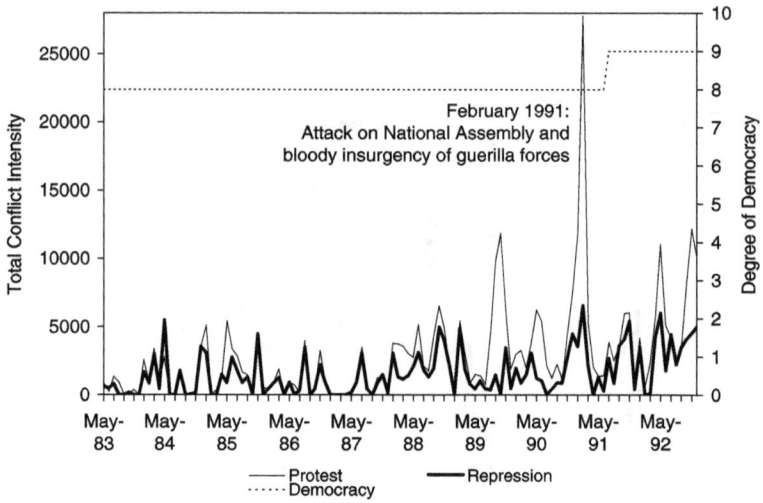

Figure A.7 Colombia, May 1983 to December 1992.

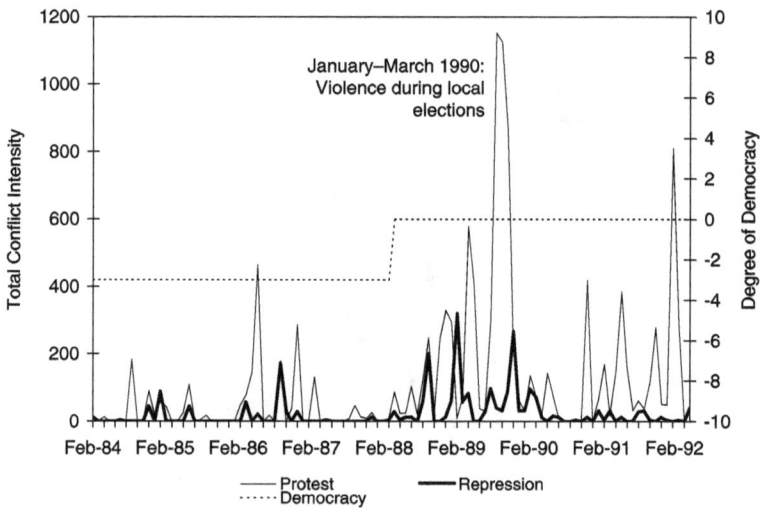

Figure A.8 Mexico, February 1984 to November 1992.

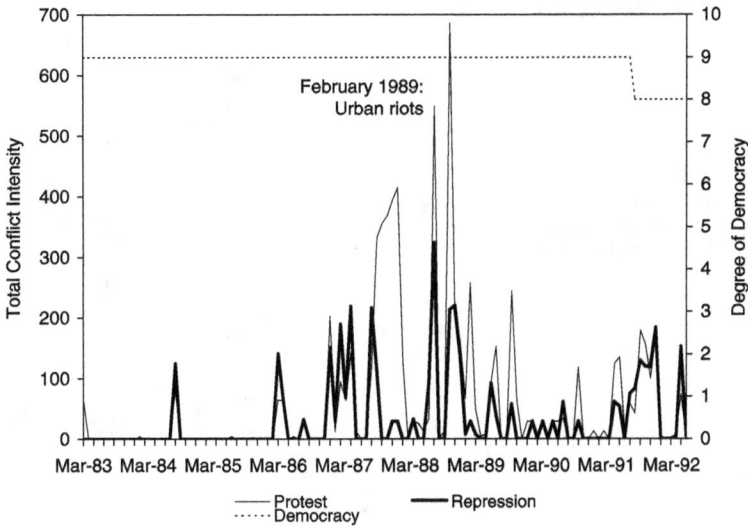

Figure A.9 Venezuela, March 1983 to December 1992.

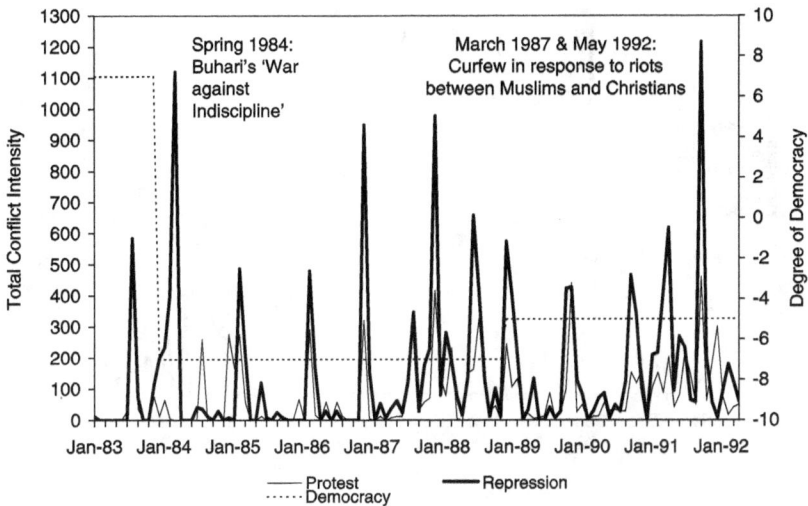

Figure A.10 Nigeria, January 1983 to December 1992.

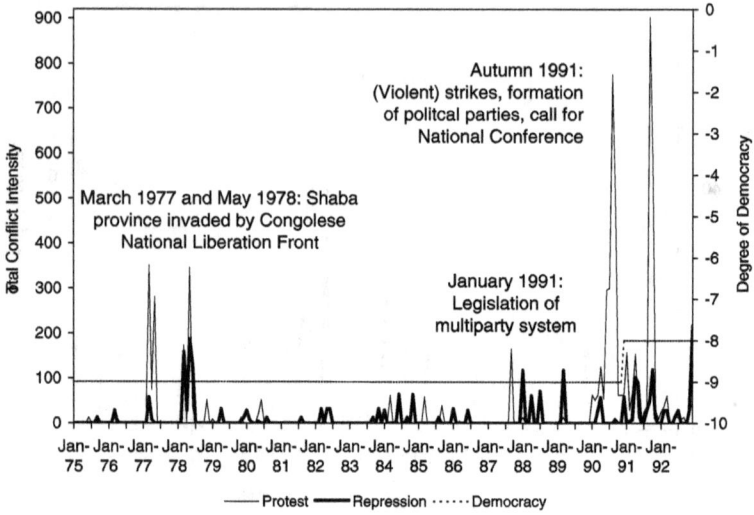

Figure A.11 Zaire, January 1974 to December 1992.

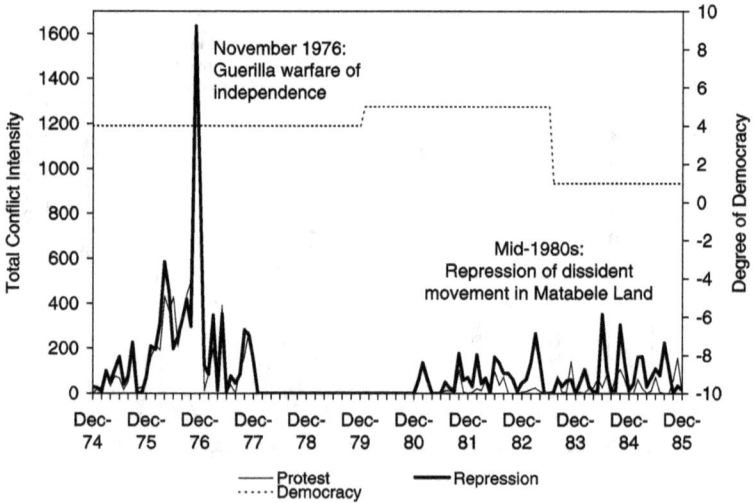

Figure A.12 Zimbabwe, December 1974 to December 1985.

References

Adams, P. (1993) 'Nigeria: Babangida's Boondoggle', in *Africa Report*, New York, July–August.

Aflatooni, A. and Allen, M.P. (1991) 'Government Sanctions and Collective Political Protest in Periphery and Semi-Periphery States: A Time-Series Analysis', *Journal of Political and Military Sociology*, 19: 29–45.

Agbaje, A. (1990) 'In Search of the Building Blocks: The State, Civil Society, Voluntary Action and Grassroots Development in Africa', *Africa Quarterly*, 30: 34–40.

Aiyede, E.R. (2003) 'The Dynamics of Civil Society and the Democratization Process in Nigeria', *Canadian Journal of African Studies/Revue Canadienne des Études Africaines*, 37: 1–27.

Arriagada, G. (1988) *Pinochet: The Politics of Power*. Boston: Unwin Hyman.

Axelrod, R. (1985) *The Evolution of Cooperation*. New York: Basic Books.

Banks, A.S. (2008) Cross-National Time-Series Data Archive User's Manual, at http://www.databanksinternational.com.

Bob, C. (2002) 'Political Process Theory and Transnational Movements: Dialectics of Protest among Nigeria's Ogoni Minority', *Social Problems*, 49: 395–415.

Booth, J.A. (1991) 'Socioeconomic and Political Roots of National Revolts in Central America', *Latin American Research Review*, 26: 33–74.

Boudreau, V. (2005) 'Precarious Regimes and Matchup Problems in the Explanation of Repressive Policy', in C. Davenport, H. Johnston and C. Mueller (eds) *Repression and Mobilization*. Minneapolis: University of Minnesota Press.

Bratton, M. and van de Walle, N. (1992) 'Popular Protest and Political Reform in Africa', *Comparative Politics*, 24: 419–42.

Bratton, M. and van de Walle, N. (1994) 'Neopatrimonial Regimes and Political Transitions in Africa', *World Politics*, 46: 453–89.

Brockett, C.D. (1991) 'The Structure of Political Opportunities and Peasant Mobilization in Central America', *Comparative Politics*, 23: 253–74.

Brysk, A. (2000) 'Democratizing Civil Society in Latin America', *Journal of Democracy*, 11: 151–65.

Buhaug, H. (2006) 'Relative Capability and Rebel Objective in Civil War', *Journal of Peace Research*, 43: 691–708.

Carey, S.C. (2006) 'The Dynamic Relationship between Protest and Repression', *Political Research Quarterly*, 59: 1–11.

Carey, S.C. (2007) 'Rebellion in Africa: Disaggregating the Effect of Political Regimes', *Journal of Peace Research*, 44: 47–64.

Carey, S.C. (2009) 'The Use of Repression as Response to Domestic Dissent', *Political Studies*, forthcoming.

Carment, D. (2003) 'Assessing State Failure: Implications for Theory and Policy', *Third World Quarterly*, 24: 407–27.

Charemza, W.W. and Deadman, D.F. (1997) *New Directions in Econometric Practice*. Cheltenham: Edward Elgar.

Chong, D. (1991) *Collective Action and the Civil Rights Movement*. Chicago: University of Chicago Press.

Cleary, M.R. (2000) 'Democracy and Indigenous Rebellion in Latin America', *Comparative Political Studies*, 33: 1123–53.

Colaresi, M. and Carey, S.C. (2008) 'To Kill or To Protect: Military Strength, Domestic Institutions, and Genocide', *Journal of Conflict Resolution*, 52: 39–67.

Collier, P. (2000) 'Doing Well Out of War: An Economic Perspective', in M. Berdal and D.M. Malone (eds) *Greed and Grievance: Economic Agendas in Civil Wars*. Boulder: Lynne Rienner.

Collier, P. and Hoeffler, A. (2004) 'Greed and Grievance in Civil War', *Oxford Economic Papers*, 56: 563–95.

Commission of Truth and Reconciliation (1991) *La Nación*. Chile.

Coser, L. (1967) *Continuities in the Study of Social Conflict*. New York: Free Press.

Crescenzi, M.J. (1999) 'Violence and Uncertainty in Transitions', *Journal of Conflict Resolution*, 43: 192–212.

Dahl, R.A. (1971) *Polyarchy: Participation and Opposition*. New Haven: Yale University Press.

Davenport, C. (1995) 'Multi-Dimensional Threat Perception and State Repression: An Inquiry into why States Apply Negative Sanctions', *American Journal of Political Science*, 39: 683–713.

Davenport, C. (1999) 'Human Rights and the Democratic Proposition', *Journal of Conflict Resolution*, 43: 92–116.

Davenport, C. (ed.) (2000) *Paths to State Repression: Human Rights Violations and Contentious Politics*. Lanham: Rowman & Littlefield.

Davenport, C. (2005) 'Introduction. Repression and Mobilization: Insights from Political Science and Sociology', in C. Davenport, H. Johnston and C. Mueller (eds) *Repression and Mobilization*. Minneapolis: University of Minnesota Press.

Davenport, C. (2007a) *State Repression and the Domestic Democratic Peace*. Cambridge: Cambridge University Press.

Davenport, C. (2007b) 'State Repression and the Tyrannical Peace', *Journal of Peace Research*, 44: 485–504.

Davenport, C. and Armstrong, D.A. (2004) 'Democracy and the Violation of Human Rights: A Statistical Analysis from 1976 to 1996', *American Journal of Political Science*, 48: 538–54.

Davenport, C., Johnston, H. and Mueller, C. (eds) (2005) *Repression and Mobilization*. Minneapolis: University of Minnesota Press.

Davies, J.C. (1962) 'Toward a Theory of Revolution', *American Sociological Review*, 27: 5–19.

Davis, D.R. and Ward, M.D. (1990) 'They Dance Alone: Deaths and the Disappeared in Contemporary Chile', *Journal of Conflict Resolution*, 34: 449–75.

Davis, D.R., Leeds, B.A. and Moore, W.H. (1998) 'Measuring Dissident and State Behavior: The Intranational Political Interactions (IPI) Project', paper presented at the Workshop on Cross-national Data Collection, Texas A&M University.

Ellina, M. and Moore, W.H. (1990) 'Discrimination and Political Violence: A Cross-National Study with Two Time Points', *Western Political Quarterly*, 43: 267–78.

Enders, W. (1995) *Applied Economic Time Series*. New York: John Wiley & Sons.

Enders, W. and Sandler, T. (1993) 'The Effectiveness of Antiterrorism Policies: A Vector-Autoregression-Intervention Analysis', *American Political Science Review*, 87: 829–44.

Fearon, J.D. and Laitin, D.D. (2003) 'Ethnicity, Insurgency, and Civil War', *American Political Science Review*, 97: 75–90.

Fein, H. (1995) 'More Murder in the Middle: Life-Integrity Violations and Democracy in the World, 1987', *Human Rights Quarterly*, 17: 170–91.

Francisco, R.A. (1995) 'The Relationship between Coercion and Protest: An Empirical Evaluation in three Coercive States', *Journal of Conflict Resolution*, 39: 263–82.

Francisco, R.A. (1996) 'Coercion and Protest: An Empirical Test in Two Democratic States', *American Journal of Political Science*, 40: 1179–204.

Freeman, J.R. (1983) 'Granger Causality and the Time Series Analysis of Political Relationships', *American Journal of Political Science*, 27: 327–58.

Freeman, J.R. (1989) 'Systematic Sampling, Temporal Aggregation and the Study of Political Relationships', *Political Analysis*, 1: 61–98.

Freeman, J.R., Williams, J.T. and Lin, T.-M. (1989) 'Vector Autoregression and the Study of Politics', *American Journal of Political Science*, 33: 842–77.

Frühling, H. (1984) 'Repressive Politics and Legal Dissent in Authoritarian Regimes: Chile 1973–1981', *International Journal of Law and Sociology*, 12: 351–74.

Garretón, M.A. (2001) 'Popular Mobilization and the Military Regime in Chile: The Complexities of the Invisible Transition', in S. Eckstein (ed.) *Power and Popular Protest: Latin American Social Movements*. Berkeley: University of California Press.

Gartner, S.S. and Regan, P.M. (1996) 'Threat and Repression: The Non-Linear Relationship between Government and Opposition Violence', *Journal of Peace Research*, 33: 273–87.

Gastil, R. (1980) *Freedom in the World: Political Rights and Civil Liberties*. Westport: Greenwood.

George, A. and Smoke, R. (1974) *Deterrence in American Foreign Policy*. New York: Columbia University Press.

Gibney, M. and Dalton, M. (1996) 'The Political Terror Scale', *Policy Studies and Developing Nations*, 4: 73–84.

Ginkel, J. and Smith, A. (1999) 'So You Say You Want a Revolution: A Game Theoretic Explanation of Revolution in Repressive Regimes', *Journal of Conflict Resolution*, 43: 291–316.

Gleditsch, N.P., Strand, H., Eriksson, M., Sollenberg, M. and Wallensteen, P. (2002) 'Armed Conflict 1946–2001: A New Dataset', *Journal of Peace Research*, 39: 615–37.

Goldstein, J.S., Pevehouse, J.C., Gerner, D.J. and Telhami, S. (2001) 'Reciprocity, Triangularity, and Cooperation in the Middle East, 1979–97', *Journal of Conflict Resolution*, 45: 594–620.

Granger, C.W.J. (1969) 'Investigating Causal Relations by Econometric Models and Cross Spectral Methods', *Econometrica*, 37: 424–38.

Greene, W.H. (2000) *Econometric Analysis*. New York: Prentice-Hall.

Gupta, D.K., Singh, H. and Sprague, T. (1993) 'Government Coercion of Dissidents', *Journal of Conflict Resolution*, 37: 301–39.

Gurr, T.R. (1968) 'Psychological Factors in Civil Violence', *World Politics*, 20: 245–78.

Gurr, T.R. (1970) *Why Men Rebel*, Princeton, Princeton University Press.

Gurr, T.R. (1986) 'Persisting Patterns of Repression and Rebellion: Foundations for a General Theory of Political Coercion', in M. Karns (ed.) *Persistent Patterns and Emergent Structures in a Waning Century*. New York: Praeger.

Gurr, T.R. (1993) *Minorities at Risk: A Global View of Ethnopolitical Conflicts*. Washington, DC: United States Institute of Peace Press.

Gurr, T.R. and Lichbach, M.I. (1986) 'Forecasting International Conflict: A Competitive Evaluation of Empirical Theories', *Comparative Political Studies*, 19: 3–38.

Hamilton, J.D. (1994) *Time Series Analysis*, Princeton: Princeton University Press.

Harbom, L., Buhaug, H., Carlsen, J. and Strand, H. (2007) UCDP/PRIO Armed Conflict Dataset Codebook, Version 4–2007. UCDP/PRIO.

Harff, B. (2003) 'No Lessons Learned from the Holocaust? Assessing Risks of Genocide and Political Mass Murder since 1955', *American Political Science Review*, 97: 57–73.

Harrelson-Stephens, J. and Callaway, R. (2003) 'Does Trade Openness Promote Security Rights in Developing Countries? Examining the Liberal Perspective', *International Interactions*, 29: 143–58.

Hegre, H. and Sambanis, N. (2006) 'Sensitivity Analysis of the Empirical Literature on Civil War Onset', *Journal of Conflict Resolution*, 50: 508–35.

Hegre, H., Ellingsen, T., Gates, S. and Gleditsch, N.P. (2001) 'Toward a Democratic Civil Peace? Democracy, Political Change, and Civil War, 1816–1992', *American Political Science Review*, 95: 33–48.

Henderson, C.W. (1991) 'Conditions Affecting the Use of Political Repression', *Journal of Conflict Resolution*, 35: 120–42.

Henderson, C.W. (1993) 'Population Pressures and Political Repression', *Social Science Quarterly*, 74: 322–33.

Herbst, J. (2000) *States and Power in Africa*. Princeton: Princeton University Press.

Hibbs, D. (1973) *Mass Political Violence*. New York: Wiley.

Hipsher, P.L. (1996) 'Democratization and the Declines of Urban Social Movements in Chile and Spain', *Comparative Politics*, 28: 273–97.

Hipsher, P.L. (1998) 'Democratic Transitions as Protest Cycles: Social Movement Dynamics in Democratizing Latin America', in D.S. Meyer and S. Tarrow (eds) *The Social Movement Society: Contentious Politics for a New Century*. Oxford: Rowman & Littlefield.

Howard, R.E. and Donnelly, J. (1986) 'Human Dignity, Human Rights, and Political Regimes', *American Political Science Review*, 80: 801–17.

Huneeus, C. (2007) *The Pinochet Regime*, Boulder: Lynne Rienner Publishers.

Huth, P. and Russett, B. (1990) 'Testing Deterrence Theory: Rigor Makes a Difference', *World Politics*, 42: 466–501.

Ihonvbere, J.O. (1996) 'Are Things Falling Apart? The Military and the Crisis of Democratisation in Nigeria', *Journal of Modern African Studies*, 34: 193–225.

Ihonvbere, J.O. and Vaughan, O. (1995) 'Nigeria: Democracy and Civil Society', in J. Wiseman, J. (ed.) *Democracy and Change in Sub-Saharan Africa*. London: Routledge.

Ikelegbe, A. (2001a) 'Civil Society, Oil and Conflict in the Niger Delta Region of Nigeria: Ramifications of Civil Society for a Regional Resource Struggle', *Journal of Modern African Studies*, 39: 437–69.

Ikelegbe, A. (2001b) 'The Perverse Manifestation of Civil Society: Evidence from Nigeria', *Journal of Modern African Studies*, 39: 1–24.

Jenkins, J.C. and Perrow, C. (1977) 'Insurgency of the Powerless: Farm Worker Movements (1946–1972)', *American Sociological Review*, 42: 249–68.

Johnston, H. and Mueller, C. (2001) 'Unobtrusive Practices of Contention in Leninist Regimes', *Sociological Perspectives*, 44: 351–75.

Kalyvas, S.N. (2006) *The Logic of Violence in Civil War*. New York: Cambridge University Press.

Khawaja, M. (1994) 'Resource Mobilization, Hardship, and Popular Collective Action in the West Bank', *Social Forces*, 73: 191–220.

Kitschelt, H. (1992) 'Political Regime Change: Structure and Process-Driven Explanations', *American Political Science Review*, 86: 1028–34.

Klandermans, B. (1984) 'Mobilization and Participation: Social-Psychological Expansion of Resource-Mobilization Theory', *American Sociological Review*, 49: 583–600.

Klandermans, B. (1997) *The Social Psychology of Protest*. Oxford: Blackwell.

Kline, H.F. (1996) 'Colombia: The Attempt to Replace Violence with Democracy,' in H.J. Wiarda and H.F. Kline (eds) *Latin American Politics and Development*. Boulder: Westview Press.

Krain, M. (1997) 'State-Sponsored Mass Murder: the Onset and Severity of Genocides and Politicides', *Journal of Conflict Resolution*, 41: 331–60.

Lawson, S. (1993) 'Conceptual Issues in the Comparative Study of Regime Change and Democratization', *Comparative Politics*, 25: 183–205.

Linz, J.J. and Stepan, A. (1996) *Problems of Democratic Transition and Consolidation: Southern Europe, South America, and Post-Communist Europe*. Baltimore: Johns Hopkins University Press.

Leng, R.J. (1984) 'Reagan and the Russians: Crisis Bargaining Beliefs and the Historical Record', *American Political Science Review*, 78: 338–55.

Lewis, P.M. (1996) 'From Prebendalism to Predation: The Political Economy of Decline in Nigeria', *Journal of Modern African Studies*, 34: 79–103.

Lewis, P.M. (1999) 'Nigeria: An End to the Permanent Transition?' *Journal of Democracy*, 10: 141–56.

Lichbach, M.I. (1987) 'Deterrence or Escalation? The Puzzle of Aggregate Studies of Repression and Dissent', *Journal of Conflict Resolution*, 31: 266–97.

Lichbach, M.I. (1995) *The Rebel's Dilemma*. Ann Arbor: University of Michigan Press.

Long, J.S. (1997) *Regression Models for Categorical and Limited Dependent Variables*. London: Sage.

McAdam, D., McCarthy, J.D. and Zald, M.N. (eds) (1996) *Comparative Perspectives on Social Movements*. New York: Cambridge University Press.

McAdam, D., Tarrow, S. and Tilly, C. (1997) 'Toward an Integrated Perspective on Social Movements and Revolution', in M.I. Lichbach and A.S. Zuckerman (eds) *Comparative Politics: Rationality, Culture, and Structure*. Cambridge: Cambridge University Press.

McAdam, D., Tarrow, S. and Tilly, C. (2001) *Dynamics of Contention*. New York: Cambridge University Press.

McCarthy, J.D. and Zald, M.N. (1977) 'Resource Mobilization and Social Movements', *American Journal of Sociology*, 82: 1212–41.

McCormick, J.M. and Mitchell, N.J. (1997) 'Human Rights Violations, Umbrella Concepts, and Empirical Analysis', *World Politics*, 49: 510–25.

McKelvey, R.D. and Zavoina, W. (1975) 'A Statistical Model for the Analysis of Ordinal Level Dependent Variables', *Journal of Mathematical Sociology*, 4: 103–20.

Macy, M.W. (1991) 'Chains of Cooperation: Threshold Effects in Collective Action', *American Sociological Review*, 56: 730–47.

Marshall, M.G. and Jaggers, K. (2001) Polity IV Project: Political Regime Characteristics and Transitions, 1800–1999. The Polity IV dataset. Vol. 2003, at http://www.systemicpeace.org/polity/polity4.htm.

Marshall, M.G. and Jaggers, K. (2002) 'Polity IV Project: Political Regime Characteristics and Transitions, 1800–2002. Dataset Users' Manual'.

Marwell, G. and Oliver, P. (1993) *The Critical Mass in Collective Action*. Cambridge: Cambridge University Press.

Mason, D.T. (2004) *Caught in the Crossfire: Revolutions, Repression, and the Rational Peasant*. Lanham: Rowman & Littlefield.

Mason, D.T. and Krane, D. (1989) 'The Political Economy of Death Squads: Toward a Theory of the Impact of State-Sanctioned Terror', *International Studies Quarterly*, 33: 175–98.

Mitchell, N.J. and McCormick, J.M. (1988) 'Economic and Political Explanations of Human Rights Violations', *World Politics*, 40: 476–98.

Moore, W.H. (1995) 'Action-Reaction or Rational Expectations? Reciprocity and the Domestic–International Conflict Nexus during the "Rhodesia Problem"', *Journal of Conflict Resolution*, 39: 129–67.

Moore, W.H. (1998) 'Repression and Dissent: Substitution, Context, and Timing', *American Journal of Political Science*, 42: 851–73.

Moore, W.H. (2000) 'The Repression of Dissent: A Substitution Model of Government Coercion', *Journal of Conflict Resolution*, 44: 107–27.

Muller, E.N. (1980) 'The Psychology of Political Protest and Violence', in T.R. Gurr (ed.) *Handbook of Political Conflict and Violence: Theory and Research*. New York: Free Press.

Muller, E.N. and Opp, K.-D. (1986) 'Rational Choice and Rebellious Collective Action', *American Political Science Review*, 80: 472–87.

Muller, E.N. and Weede, E. (1990) 'Cross-National Variations in Political Violence: A Rational Action Approach', *Journal of Conflict Resolution*, 34: 642–51.

Muller, E.N. and Weede, E. (1994) 'Theories of Rebellion: Relative Deprivation and Power Contention', *Rationality and Society*, 6: 40–57.

Myers, D.J. (1996) 'Venezuela: The Stressing of Distributive Justice', in H.J. Wiarda and H.F. Kline (eds) *Latin American Politics and Development*. Boulder: Westview Press.

Oberschall, A. (1993) *Social Movements, Ideologies, Interests, and Identities*. New Brunswick: Transaction Publishers.

Oberschall, A. (1994) 'Rational Choice in Collective Protests', *Rationality and Society*, 6: 79–100.

Olson, M. (1993) 'Dictatorship, Democracy, and Development', *American Political Science Review*, 87: 567–76.

Opp, K.-D. (1994) 'Repression and Revolutionary Action: East Germany in 1989', *Rationality and Society*, 6: 101–38.

Opp, K.-D. and Roehl, W. (1990) 'Repression, Micromobilization, and Political Protest', *Social Forces*, 69: 521–47.

Osaghae, E.E. (1995) 'The Ogoni Uprising: Oil Politics, Minority Agitation and the Future of the Nigerian State', *African Affairs*, 94: 325–44.

Oxhorn, P. (1994) 'Where Did All the Protesters Go? Popular Mobilization and the Transition to Democracy in Chile', *Latin American Perspectives*, 21: 49–68.

Oxhorn, P. (1995) *Organizing Civil Society: The Popular Sectors and the Struggle for Democracy in Chile*. University Park: Pennsylvania State University Press.

Pierce, D.A. (1977) 'Relationships – and Lack thereof – between Economic Time Series, with Special Reference to Money and Interest Rates', *Journal of the American Statistical Association*, 72: 11–22.

Piven, F.F. and Cloward, R.A. (1995) 'Collective Protest: A Critique of Resource-Mobilization Theory', in S.M. Lyman (ed.) *Social Movements: Critiques, Concepts, Case Studies*. London: Macmillan.

Poe, S.C. (2004) 'The Decision to Repress: An Integrative Theoretical Approach to the Research on Human Rights and Repression', in S.C. Carey and S.C. Poe (eds) *Understanding Human Rights Violations: New Systematic Studies*. Aldershot: Ashgate.

Poe, S.C. and Tate, C.N. (1994) 'Repression of Human Rights and Personal Integrity in the 1980s: A Global Analysis', *American Political Science Review*, 88: 853–72.

Poe, S.C., Carey, S.C. and Vazquez, T.M. (2001) 'How are these Pictures Different? A Quantitative Comparison of the US State Department and Amnesty International Human Rights Reports, 1976–1995', *Human Rights Quarterly*, 23: 650–77.

Poe, S.C., Rost, N. and Carey, S.C. (2006) 'Assessing Risk and Opportunity in Conflict Studies: A Human Rights Analysis', *Journal of Conflict Resolution*, 50: 1–24.

Poe, S.C., Tate, C.N. and Camp Keith, L. (1999) 'Repression of the Human Right to Personal Integrity Revisited: A Global Cross-National Study covering the Years 1976–1993', *International Studies Quarterly*, 43: 291–313.

Rasler, K.A. (1996) 'Concessions, Repression, and Political Protest in the Iranian Revolution', *American Sociological Review*, 61: 132–52.

Regan, P.M. and Henderson, E.A. (2002) 'Democracy, Threats and Political Repression in Developing Countries: Are Democracies Internally Less Violent?' *Third World Quarterly*, 23: 119–36.

Richards, D.L., Gelleny, R.D. and Sacko, D.H. (2001) 'Money with a Mean Streak? Foreign Economic Penetration and Government Respect for Human Rights in Developing Countries', *International Studies Quarterly*, 45: 219–39.

Rothchild, D. (1991) 'An Interactive Model for State-Ethnic Relations', in F.M. Deng and I.W. Zartman (eds) *Conflict Resolution in Africa*. Washington, DC: Brookings Institution.

Rule, J.B. (1988) *Theories of Civil Violence*. Berkeley: University of California Press.

Rummel, R.J. (1997) *Power Kills: Democracy as a Method of Nonviolence*. New Brunswick: Transaction Books.

Salazar, G. (1990) *Violencia Política Popular en las 'Grandes Alamedas'*, SUR, Santiago, Chile.

Schatzman, C. (2005) 'Political Challenge in Latin America: Rebellion and Collective Protest in an Era of Democratization', *Journal of Peace Research*, 42: 291–310.

Schneider, C.L. (1995) *Shantytown Protest in Pinochet's Chile*. Philadelphia: Temple University Press.

Shellman, S.M. (2004) 'Measuring the Intensity of Intranational Political Interactions Event Data: Two Interval-Like Scales', *International Interactions*, 30: 109–41.

Sims, C. (1980) 'Macroeconomics and Reality', *Econometrica*, 48: 1–49.

Sims, C. (1987) 'Vector Autoregressions and Reality: Comment', *Journal of Business and Economic Statistics*, 5: 443–9.

Sommer, H. and Scarritt, J.R. (1999) 'The Utility of Reuters for Events Analysis in Area Studies: The Case of Zambia–Zimbabwe Interactions, 1982–1993', *International Interactions*, 25: 29–59.

Stohl, M. and Carleton, D. (1985) 'The Foreign Policy of Human Rights: Rhetoric and Reality from Jimmy Carter to Ronald Reagan', *Human Rights Quarterly*, 7: 205–29.

Sutter, D. (1995) 'Settling Old Scores: Potholes along the Transition from Authoritarian Rule', *Journal of Conflict Resolution*, 39: 110–28.

Swaminathan, S. (1999) 'Time, Power, and Democratic Transitions', *Journal of Conflict Resolution*, 43: 178–91.

Tarrow, S. (1991) 'Struggle, Politics, and Reform: Collective Action, Social Movements, and Cycles of Protest', in *Cornell Western Societies Paper no. 21*. Ithaca: Cornell University Press.

Tarrow, S. (1994) *Power in Movement: Social Movements, Collective Action and Politics*. Cambridge: Cambridge University Press.

Tarrow, S. (1995) 'Cycles of Collective Action: Between Movements of Madness and the Repertoires of Contention', in M. Traugott (ed.) *Repertoires and Cycles of Collective Action*. Durham: Duke University Press.

Taylor, M. (1998) 'Rationality and Revolutionary Collective Action', in M. Taylor (ed.) *Rationality and Revolution*. Cambridge: Cambridge University Press.

Tilly, C. (1978) *From Mobilization to Revolution*. New York: McGraw-Hill.

Tilly, C. (1984) *Big Structures, Large Processes, Huge Comparisons*. New York: Russell Sage Foundation.

Weinstein, J.M. (2007) *Inside Rebellion: The Politics of Insurgent Violence*. Cambridge: Cambridge University Press.

Wiseman, J. (1986) 'Urban Riots in West Africa, 1977–1985', *Journal of Modern African Studies*, 24: 509–18.

Zanger, S. C. (2000) 'The Global Analysis of the Effect of Political Regime Changes on Life Integrity Violations, 1977–93', *Journal of Peace Research*, 37: 213–33.

Zielinski, J. (1999) 'Transitions from Authoritarian Rule and the Problem of Violence', *Journal of Conflict Resolution*, 43: 213–28.

Zimmerman, E. (1980) 'Macro-Comparative Research on Political Protest', in T.R. Gurr (ed.) *Handbook of Political Conflict: Theory and Research*. New York: Free Press.

Index

For Product Safety Concerns and Information please contact our EU
representative GPSR@taylorandfrancis.com
Taylor & Francis Verlag GmbH, Kaufingerstraße 24, 80331 München, Germany